netting
the
flow

Cover Painting *'The Ghost Hole' by James Cooke*

ISBN 0-9548251-3-6

An **OSWICA** *publication - contact gerry.m@nireland.com*

Printed by The Universities Press (Belfast) Ltd

Supported by the National Lottery 'Awards for All'

Introduction

The Comber Reading and Creative Writing groups were formed in 2005 in response to a desire among local people to share the experiences of some of their favourite pastimes.

Meeting monthly in Comber Library has enabled the members to benefit from collective wisdom brought to hobbies that are in essence of a solitary nature.

The regular discussions have been enhanced by a variety of projects – such as old film footage of the Comber area from the Northern Ireland Film Archives, a private showing of the latest 'Pride and Prejudice' film, a talk by and discussion with the writer Jennifer Johnston, and writing workshops in Castle Espie and Scrabo Tower.

The collection contains pieces which were written under the pressure of 10-minute workshops as well as items which the writers have refined over a period of time.

The Reading Group has contributed a review of an established local classic 'December Bride' and an interview with local author David Park.

In this book of literary pieces we hope to give members an opportunity to showcase their various talents and interests. We trust that there is something here to suit all tastes, and that the discerning readers will appreciate those pieces which appeal to them without being too critical of those which are not to their liking.

We would like to express our gratitude –
to the *South Eastern Education and Library Board* and the staff of Comber Library for the help and support which they give us;
to the *Ards Borough Council Arts Committee* for their financial support; and
to the *National Lottery 'Awards for All'* programme which has made this publication possible.

CONTENTS

Foreword

Thirty years ago, just after the publication of my first book, I invited
entries for a short story competition from writers in the Ards and Comber
area. We got four entries from the Peninsula and its groin.

Ten years later I was sitting in the teachers' room in a County Down
school, waiting to address P6-7, when I was approached by a teacher
whose bilious appearance and nicotine-stained fingers marked him out as
a deputy headmaster who had failed three headship interviews.

Before an audience of half a dozen of his colleagues he tried to dim my
sparkle by way of the following broadside:

" About ten years ago I entered one of your short story competitions; I
crammed and cluttered it with every cliché,platitude and bromide that I
could think up…"

He paused, then went for the thrapple:

"I won the first prize," he said.

"Oh,yes," I said, "I think I recall it."

I gave him a sunny smile: I know the ways of some teachers.

On another occasion in the same circumstances in Belfast a schoolmaster
said to me:"We got your message that you couldn't make it yesterday
because you were filming with RTE. We were impressed."

"That's enough about me," I said," let's change the subject: what did you
think of my last book?"

To the County Down teacher I explained, truthfully:

"The thing about it was, we only got four entries and yours came first.
Compared to the other three, your work looked as tight as Hemingway's."

But that was long ago.

Now Comber and Newtownards and all the way up and down the
Peninsula they're giving West Belfast, Downpatrick, Armagh and Tommy
Sands' country a run for their money.

It's a pleasure to see the name of Comber Reading and Creative Writing
Group on this collection.

The arts are strong in and all round this town: I have a nice oil painting of
Scrabo Tower by Jennifer Graham above my seat by the fire, I have four
collections by the Ards Writers'Group on my shelves and now I can add
one under the name of my home town.

All in all, this collection by local writers is a most interesting and enjoyable
one, covering a wide range of creative endeavour, and the nicest thing for
me about it is that, from the look of these works, as the Belfast comedian
Jimmy Cricket likes to say: "And there's more!"

Sam McAughtry

Nasturtiums

Clearing up the garden a thought occurred -
Why no poems about nasturtiums?
Paeans of praise for pansies and poppies,
The humble daisy lauded by the Bard himself.
Has no-one noticed that when all is closing down
Rose and lily fade,
Great towers of hollyhocks collapse
And sunflowers droop o'er spires of willowherb
The golden glory of nasturtiums cascades and climbs on walls
Casts canopies o'er empty spaces and
Clothes desolation in splendid tints of autumn?
Rich golds and bronzes
Vivid crimsons, blazing orange and sunlit yellows
Challenge the rusted hedgerows and glowing orchards.
Overwhelming in its amplitude.
No vapid pinks nor misty lavenders
To dim the celebration.
Tangy leaves no less munificent
Shining with silver snail trails
Leave intricate lacework.
Only icy fingers of first frost can kill
This blaze of affluence.
But rich harvests of seedpods remain,
An encore for far-off future summers.

Eirene Armstrong

The Young Bride
by
Jean Galway

When I was a young bride my father asked me what I would like for a Christmas present. I'm sure he didn't imagine for a moment that I would ask for some good laying hens

A few weeks later a very sturdy henhouse arrived, followed soon afterwards by a dozen lovely white wyandottes. I was delighted. My husband fixed perches and a dropping board, while I lined six orange boxes with straw for nesting boxes. We were soon rewarded by the first eggs. Is there anything to beat fresh free-range eggs? The twelve hens were useful for clearing up leftover cooked potatoes and stale bread, which I mixed with their meal. I used to love seeing them dusting themselves in the dry earth in the space below the henhouse, which was raised off the ground by cement blocks.

One day there was a heavy shower and the hens were all under the henhouse, either sheltering from the rain or perhaps moulding themselves. I came out as usual with their hot mash, and to make sure I was emptying the bucket of all its contents I brought the rim of it down with a heavy thud on the ground. At that very moment one of the hens flew out from under the henhouse and the full force of the heavy bucket crushed its neck. The hen wasn't killed cleanly, instantly, but staggered about for a few moments before dropping dead.

My heart had stopped for a moment when I saw what I had done to one of my loved and lovely white hens. I felt sick, really sick, and oppressed by guilt. When people say that so and so was running around like a headless chicken, I wonder if they have ever seen one. Every time, even to this day, that I hear that phrase I feel nearly as sick as I did that day.

When Alex came home from work I poured out the story of the dead hen. "But Jean, it was a perfectly healthy bird, and it met with a clean death. It'll be all right for eating."

"No, no, " I shouted, "I'm not going to cook it."

Alex plucked the hen just the same, and gave it to a neighbour. It was better than having to bury it, and anyway, I suppose, it was a case of an ill wind blowing somebody good. As for me, I was squeamish for weeks afterwards, and went off chicken.

That was one period in my life when I could easily have been persuaded to become a vegetarian......

The House

Four corners made of brick and two bay windows
Either side of door, beneath a sloping roof.
Standing bravely, smiling in the sun,
Or crouching in rain with shoulders round.
This is the house, chimneys pointing towards the sky.
A garden stretches out before, grass grown tall,
And hedge around guards all. A driveway passes
Up to the front door, which painted red, peeling,
Stands sentinel on the step, leading to tiled hall.
Stairs rise to a bathroom, off a landing which
Leads to bedrooms, four set above a large reception
With two more to front and rear and a tiny kitchen,
Minute to modern eye, completes the structure.
A garden to the rear grows currants, apples
And many coloured flowers, whose blooms
Attract noisy bees and insects in the sun.
A family lived here, their dramatic lives
Of laughter and tears as years changed.
The young grew up to leave like fledglings.
Their parents stayed till death arrived.
Dumb walls remained, keeping their secrets.
Glass crunches, from a picture frame, showing
They were here, a lonely symbol.
Only cold draught of air from empty windows
Chills like death, not even ghosts remain.

Ray Heath

The Spider

I found a spider in the bath.
A big one,
Trapped there in vast whiteness.
Picking him up on a magazine
I carried him to the window.
He didn't want to go;
Scurrying along the windowsill
He hid behind the deodorant.
From his crouching stance
I knew he was adamant.
And so I let him stay.

Ray Heath

Self is Cool

Self is cool
I searched in university
It wasn't as I'd read
Like Oxford's elongated bods cloistering for an edge
Like ripples to infinity,
Like snakes in lemon grass,
'Twas more a million bluebottles
Crammed on a Golden Ass.

Self is cool
I searched for it in Voluntary work
Growing full of hedges
Community development – suturing the edges
Like dancing in Divinity,
Like blackbirds losing plumage,
'Twas more a million willing steers
Branded with an image.

Self is soul
I searched for it in Language,
Where poetry is mighty,
Where Soul's synoptic reasoning is aiming for a birdie
Like touching in the moment,
Like rhythmic continuity,
'Twas more a million jigging puns
Bristling through my nightie.

Self is soul
I search for it in family
Where self has ever been
Where Holly, Adam, Leigh and Joel are hotting up the scene
Like swimming in a heated sea
Like carpets on oak flooring,
'Twas more a myriad of boats
On one solitary mooring.

Cool is God
I give thanks every day,
For giving me a thirsty soul with attitude and will
But now I'm dozing in my chair, God keep my soul
Until...........

Dorothy Pyper

Grandfather's Delight
by
William Fitzell

Dedicated to my grandchildren Rachael, Jacob Bethyn and Sarah

Big John sat upright in his armchair and snuffed out his pipe before he emptied the smouldering tobacco into the grate and carefully placed it on the mantelpiece. The commotion caused by little John, as he came rushing up the garden path leading to his thatched cottage, had alerted the big man that the visit he had been looking forward to had arrived. Bursting into the living room, yards ahead of his mother, shouting, "Grandpa", the boy threw himself into the waiting arms of his adoring Grandfather for the 'bear hug' he loved. They were buddies, best friends, and mates. This was the highlight of the week for both of them.

The cottage, idyllic as it was, had become a lonely place for big John since his wife died. Her passing had left him feeling wounded. When he looked across the hearth at the empty chair opposite, he was reminded of the emptiness her passing had left in his life. It seemed nothing could compensate him for his loss. Left alone with his grief he had found it difficult to get on with the normal business of living. The days, the nights and the weeks grew longer as time passed while his interest in things and people around him diminished. All he had to look forward to was these weekend visits of his daughter and grandson. The arrival of little John had ignited a fresh spark of life in the old man; at weekends he felt young again. As the boy grew and his fondness for him became stronger he looked forward to these visits, recognizing, they lifted him, if only for a short while, out of his depression.

"Mary, get the kettle on while I sort out milk and ginger snaps for us men." She was already heading for the kitchen. Calling on her father meant as much to her as it did to her son. Seeing him sparkle like this made these visits something she had to do.

"Where are we going to-day, grandpa?" asked little John, as he nibbled his biscuit. They never wasted time indoors but took themselves off on a journey of discovery, along one country lane or another.

"I think", replied grandpa, "I think we'll head for Archer's farm. What do you say to that, me lad?" he asked, as he playfully ruffled the boy's shock of golden curls. Already little John was excited.

"Will we need pencil and paper, grandpa?"

"No, lad, all we'll need is a sharp ear, a keen eye and an inquisitive mind. Have you got those now?" he asked with a smile as he gave him a friendly poke in the ribs. The boy giggled. The fun had already begun.

Mary quietly noted everything that went on between them as she went about the cottage, doing her own things, watching them 'gel' as they geared up for the outing. She never discovered what went on between them when they took themselves off like this. When they left they were bubbling over with anticipation and when they returned they were happy and contented. Asking questions, in an attempt to uncover what transpired between the pair when they were gone, never worked. It was their world and she respected that. Astutely, she watched for signs that her father had recovered from the grief that had lingered with him for such a long time. His cupboards and fridge were poorly stocked. She could see he had lost weight. He never took a holiday or travelled into town unless it was absolutely necessary; he had lost touch with his friends and neighbours, something that would never have happened when her mother was alive. The time for trying to share his grief by talking had long passed. Feeling there was nothing else she could do she was always there for him. Settled in the armchair, with a cup of tea and her library book, she turned to respond to their loud bye-byes as they hurried out the cottage door, with a wave, a smile and an order to behave themselves. How her father managed to deal with the stream of questions that kept coming from the boy's fertile mind, she could only guess. She didn't have the answers to many things, but as a mother she could see her boy growing in confidence with every visit. Spending time with his Grandfather like this was good for him.

Little John danced ahead of his Grandfather, skipping, first to one side of the road and skipping back again, like a spring lamb, happy being alive. Big John was sure he heard the boy singing. His capacity for enjoyment was growing, but this was a new dimension to his expression of delight. It was all so natural. He would have joined in the song, if only he knew the words, instead he contented himself watching his grandson with a pride and a tenderness that surprised him. They hadn't gone far when it seemed mother nature had opened her arms to embrace them, invitingly beckoning them on, as if wanting to share her secrets. Relaxed, and in total harmony with his surroundings, the old man opened himself up, willing himself to enjoy the experience, feeling the innocence of the boy dancing ahead of him without inhibition. There was so much that was wholesome being in his company, walking in the country lanes where it was warm and clean, fresh and bright, colourful and full of wonder. He couldn't imagine what was in store for them that afternoon but sensed this was going to be one of their better days out together.

"Come on, lad, we better get motoring, there's a lot to see at Archer's" With that word he took the lead and as he strode out there was a lightness in his step as he looked around him seeing the countryside through the eyes of the child. He lived in the middle of all this beauty but when his grandson joined him on these trips it was as if he were enjoying creation for the first time. The sun rising in the blue sky held a welcoming warmth that wasn't there on lonely days; the green fields glistened with a lushness as if the almighty had fed and watered the whole world just for them; hedgerows and trees provided shelter for birds that filled the air with full throated song, as if to greet them. Such was the wonder of the rolling countryside, home to cattle; sheep; horses; pigs; clucking hens and quacking ducks. Giant oaks and spreading chestnuts provided an umbrella where bluebells, wild daffodils and crocuses bloomed in profusion. Tall firs stood like sentinels on long driveways leading to farm houses protected by giant pines from winter squalls. Willows lined the banks of a stream as it meandered down from the hills before finding its way into the river below. The air was sharp while light breezes carried odours of farm life across the hedgerows, each odour carrying with it its own story. The barking of collies was a constant reminder that life on the farm was always busy, just out of view of the passer by. As big John took all this in, he was at peace with himself. 'This is God's classroom', he thought.

His reverie was interrupted by a shout of glee from little John. "Grandpa.!! We're here, grandpa!! Look!!" Running to his side the boy placed his little hand into that of his Grandfather's while pointing to the sign by the road, 'Archer's Farm. 100 yards.' The old man never felt as good as he did just at that moment; such was the bond that existed between them. There never was a lot of talk; there was no bartering; no inducements; no rules; no reprimands and no reminders about who was boss. Their comradeship grew out of mutual love. Who gained most from the relationship was never the issue. The only thing that mattered was that nothing could possibly spoil what they shared. When at home in his cottage, sitting by the log fire in the evenings with his pipe in hand and in a reflective mood, he wondered about the thing that bound them together. A pragmatic man, he was certainly no philosopher, he knew there was no escaping that what he felt for his grandson was like nothing he had ever known. Any attempt, to define or explain it would result in something being lost in the telling. So he never tried, not even to Mary. Could it be that he had to wait almost seventy years to discover something as rare as this! Had he rediscovered his own childhood! What of the feelings he had known for his late wife, and his daughter? These could not be denied, but neither could anyone deny that he and the boy were very close. What they had, he felt, was love plus something. It was that indefinable something, that made the difference between the ordinary and the extraordinary. Of one thing he was sure, whatever years remained to him, watching his grandson grow, would fill him with pride and he would end his days happy to have been little John's 'Grandpa.'

"Look, lad, up on the top field, the tractor, can you see it? The boy climbed to the top of the five bar gate for a better view.
"Is he ploughing, grandpa?"
"Bright lad. Now can you tell me why he's ploughing?"
"He's going to sow seed, grandpa."
"Right again, it's the time for sowing and planting. Can you tell me what happens next?" Little John hesitated just long enough to allow his Grandfather to answer his own question. "Well, son, just as there is a time for sowing so there will come a time for reaping. The rain and sun help the seed to grow until a harvest is produced. When that time comes the farmer will use his other big machine, the combine harvester, the one with the

great big blades, and cut the crop and store it in his barn before sending it
to market." Little John was following his Grandfather closely.
"What will the harvest be, grandfather?"
"He'll reap what he sows son. If he sows wheat, the harvest will be wheat.
If he sows barley the harvest will be barley. The farmer gets back exactly
what he puts into the soil." Little John was now warming to this lively
exchange.
"Is there always a harvest, grandpa?"
"There will always be a harvest lad as long as God sends the sun and the
rain to make the seed to grow." The big man helped the boy down from
his perch on top of the gate and the pair continued further up the lane to
where a flock of sheep was softly grazing. As they walked together big
John continued the 'lesson'.
"You see, son, it's the same in life; as with the farmer and his sowing, you
get back what you sow. Sow love, you get love coming back to you, or,
make others happy you can be sure happiness will be your reward.
Enough about the ploughing the sowing and the reaping, let's look at
these sheep"
   Arriving at a break in the hedge they had a close view of a ewe and her
lamb.
"That lamb can't be more than a few hours old, it's not often town dwellers
like us get to see one so young." Soon the lamb was struggling to its feet,
tottering, wobbling, falling and struggling back to its feet again, bleating
with every failed attempt to steady itself, until finally it succeeded,
finding, as it did so, shelter, protection and nourishment beneath its
mother. Excited by what he was seeing the boy kept firing questions at his
Grandpa.
"This is what springtime is all about, son; it's the time for new life, new
beginnings, when lambs are born."
"How long will the lamb live, grandpa?" The big man thought before
answering.
 "Well" he said, "hopefully she will grow to be a fine sheep like her mother
and have babies just like her. Then the time will come when she will die."
Little John was quick with his next question.
"Does she have to die, grandpa?"
"Yes, lad, just as there is a time to be born there is a time to die."
"Just like grandma had to die?" asked little John, with a gentleness that
surprised his Grandfather who felt his heart had been touched and
reassured in that moment. Then, in muted tones, almost as if speaking to
himself, he echoed the words of the boy.
"Just like grandma had to die." Even as he spoke, he choked on the words
and a solitary tear moistened the corner of his eye, before gently rolling
down his cheek. A lull descended on the exchange of question and answer
between man and boy, just enough time to allow a healing balm to settle
on his spirit. He recalled the words of the wise man 'out of the mouths of
babes comes forth wisdom.' He was glad he'd had this encounter.

Mary was waiting for them at the door when they returned. Little John came bouncing up the path and into the cottage, just ahead of his Grandfather.

"I'm hungry, Mum"

"Dinner will be ready soon." As she spoke she stole a furtive glance at her father who seemed quieter than usual on returning from their Saturday morning excursion. She decided not to pry but wait until they chose to share with her whatever it was went on between them while they were gone. They were hungry and soon cleaned their plates. Washing-up done, it was time for mother and son to leave. The boy got his hug from his Grandfather, then, turning to his daughter, he held her in his arms and whispered in her ear;

"It's over, Mary; I'm okay now. You don't need to worry about me any more."

She understood.

The Old Oak Tree

I have stood here, solid, dependable, enduring,
on this same spot, three centuries and more.
My spreading branches shelter for weary travellers,
my bosom sanctuary for wild life in the wet.

Strong sinewed fibre from my kith and kin
has built one thousand ships and more,
craft that explored exotic lands, took men to wars,
yet in peace crowned grand cathedrals reaching heavenwards.

My maturity testifies to Nature's wonder,
from forest loam's acorn to sapling young,
a weedy sapling starved of light,
but Nature in her wisdom regulates all growth.

Some three centuries and more ago
the ringing of the axe was heard:
a great oak felled, I mourned its passing.
but energised by light I reached for sky.

I stand here now, safe from woodsman's axe,
protected, living proof to our great history,
a thing of beauty that people touch, admire.
I am king of these woods, I am the oak.

Tom Jamison

The Bluebell Wood

The magic of the bluebell wood
Has filled my heart with joy
The azure perfumed carpet
Spread like a shining sea.
No careless foot has trodden here
To crush these fragile blooms.
In silent awe, I deeply breathe
This heady perfumed air
And wish that I could bottle some
To remind me of this day and place.

Jean Galway

That's Nature
by
Jean Hinds

It was early May, not too warm or showery, with birds busy looking for
the material to prepare nets for their new families, while some were more
advanced and already feeding their newly-born. Spring had arrived.
I noticed a male blackbird sitting on the fence and sounding most
annoyed.   I thought a cat or dog must be too close for comfort but then I
noticed that another bird was lying motionless on the ground – it was the
female blackbird.
I lifted it gently, hoping that it was just stunned, but it had broken its neck
when it had flown into the window.
How sad, I thought, just like humans raising a family and one left to cope
with everything when the other dies.
Does he feel grief, I wondered as I hoped that he would continue to feed
and nurture his young family.
Next year will he find another mate and start all over again?
Isn't that what nature is all about?

A Big Man

From the moment we met I admired the man –
cool and decisive and commanding respect
from all whom he met –
except his dog, which refused to respond
to any order he barked (not the dog but the man).

The first meal that we shared with two interpreters,
- although I often wondered how much
he actually understood without them -
was punctuated by many stories of
the tough life on a farm in the country
fifty years before.

The most vivid description I recall quite clearly
as he enjoyed watching me squirm
at the intricate details of a family occasion
when everyone gathered to watch
the ritual slaughter
of a pig that was almost a pet.

And others I will not mention at all.

The simple city boy under the spell of the country giant.

Years later when we met for the annual meal
I recounted the episodes of that first occasion
as I clearly remembered them all –
the pig that was almost a pet
and others I will not mention at all.

Some he remembered and others not –
at least he said that was so.
The pig story was true, others perhaps,
and one he denied to have happened.

Was the simple city boy under the spell of the giant once more?
Was the palinka playing tricks on the mind?
Who was imagining the stories denied –
and rats I will not mention at all?

Gerry Miller

Interview with local writer **David Park**

'Oranges from Spain', a volume of short stories, set against the background of the Troubles, was first published in the 1980's. Since then David Park has written five novels **'The Healing'**, **'The Rye Man'**, **'Stone Kingdoms'**, **'The Big Snow'** and **'Swallowing the Sun'**. A teacher, he lives in County Down with his wife Alberta and their two children. That much we can find from the publisher but I was interested in finding out more about this local author. I have read his books and especially love the brilliant imagery that he brings to his writing. David kindly agreed to answer some of my questions and I hope that you, the reader, will be encouraged to pick up one - if not all - of his novels.

How does your writing process take place?

I wait until I'm sure I have a book to write. Different ideas come but I have to let them swirl around the mind before I write the first word. If I set out on the wrong idea then it's a huge amount of time wasted. Sometimes you try to tell yourself that the idea is right when really you know it's wrong. Sooner or later you are forced to acknowledge the truth. I always try to make it sooner. I know the start of the story and I usually know the ending. The bit in between evolves and grows. I don't plan rigidly. I don't write any type of plan down. A book needs to be allowed to shape itself to some degree, it can't all be predetermined. The structure, however, is important and that has to be clear early on. I try to make myself write a set number of words per session. I just keep plodding on, hoping my instinct is taking me in the right direction. The one thing I know is that nothing happens until I actually start to write

Which of your books gave you the most satisfaction to write?

I don't often dwell on past books and I never go back to them after they're written. There is an element of fear in this because I'm probably frightened that they'll disappoint me and when they're out in the world it's too late to call them back to try and remedy real or imagined imperfections. This feeling of apprehension is both a positive and a negative because it's the constant dissatisfaction that acts as the spur to try and try again. So when I'm asked about favourite books, the truth is that there are only books that dissatisfy me less than others. If I'm pushed I'd say I feel some affection for Stone Kingdoms. It's less read perhaps but it's the book where I stretched imaginatively further than I had done before. The African setting, the fact that the narrator is female, all contributed to a new sense of risk taking as a writer.

.

What are your future writing plans?

I've just completed a new novel for Bloomsbury which will possibly be called Troubling the Waters. It's also going to be published in America. It describes four contrasting lives in Northern Ireland, their preoccupations and dilemmas, and then how these four lives come to be linked once more through a shared moment in their past.

'The Big Snow' is on our reading list for next year. Will you be happy with this as our first choice?
Perhaps some of the group might remember this particular event. Others will be too young possibly. But age doesn't really matter. I wrote the book mostly in July and August. It's not easy writing about snow in the summer! The book is a series of interrelated stories that echo each other and are set against a backdrop of the Arctic weather that paralysed the country but also gave it a mysterious and temporary beauty.

Eileen Ferguson

The Teacher

Like a dog, like a dog they could no longer love
She crept to her bed, curling in a spiral.
Once she'd been a ball that they could throw and fetch
At will
Something was missing some undone thing had left an edge.
She searched for it day and night, night and day in her head in her bed
Until it came to her
Suddenly
Like from the desert
There arose a tiny spring, a water thing that spouted in the air and wet the ground
Around.
She became so busy trying to direct the flow into
Useable vessels
She forgot what they were at, turning on her now unleavened legs,
She pushed a few seeds
Deep into the ground.
And found herself making another garden.

Dorothy Pyper

A Rat's Revenge
by
Eddie Whiteside

The apprentice's boots scraped the top of the wooden box as, with
difficulty, he assumed a squatting position, which he hoped would keep
him safely off the ground. In front of him in the courtyard, in a semi-
circle of human expectancy, had gathered the shipyard workers,who were
hurriedly summoned, each hoping to be the one to get a kick in.
'Are youse all ready?' he screamed, his face contorted with excitement.
The inevitable, unanimous 'Yeah!' chorused back to the gargoyle-like
figure, who slowly raised the side panel of the box.
The rat scurried out.
Jimmy, the master carpenter who had helped his apprentice design and
make the box, wondered if he had done the right thing in not disposing of
the rat in the usual way, by drowning it in the big water tank. He had
succumbed to his apprentice's pleas to 'give it a chance', persuading
himself that his motive had something to do with an act of kindness. Now,
as he gazed at the surreal scene before him, he was filled with foreboding.
The rodent saw the hostile crowd in front of it and immediately turned
and scuttled in the opposite direction. As it passed him still perched on his
box,a shriek went up from the apprentice. Whooping and yelling like
Apaches the mob immediately chased after it and, in panic, the rat darted
into a very narrow, dead-end entry between two buildings. A couple of
large, parallel, heating pipes ran the length of the cul-de-sac at ground
level.
The crowd stopped at the entrance. A strange silence descended on them,
reflecting their uncertainty on how to proceed. Had their victim escaped?
Was it still in there?
Jimmy gazed briefly into the gloom of the entry, trying to figure out what
to do next. Placing one foot on each pipe, he waddled his way up their
length, peering down between his legs as he went. There it was, huddled
against the wall in a corner, as far away as it could get. He went back and
collected a heavy, metal hammer from one of the onlookers.
'When I drop this hammer, it'll come running out. Get ready to finish it.'
Before he could say any more, the apprentice ran up and tugged him by
the sleeve.
'Can I come?'
Jimmy struggled to suppress a sigh of exasperation, but just nodded
assent.
'Don't drop it 'til I'm ready,' said the apprentice.
Jimmy went along the pipes first. The apprentice followed him a few feet
into the entry and then stopped. He turned and leaned his back against
one wall and pushed his feet up against the opposite wall until his knees
were tucked almost under his chin. He sought safety in being as high
above the rat as possible. In this gravity-defying position he shouted 'Ready!'

The hammer dropped and, as planned, the rat came racing out. It plummeted along underneath the apprentice and out into the yard. There was a sudden, noisy surge forward from the onlookers, followed by some shoving and skipping. In the melee the rat successfully negotiated two or three swipes from hefty boots, before one well-aimed kick caught it square on the head. Its lifeless body flew in a graceful arc into the air, turning and twisting, tumbling and somersaulting, trailing blood, for all the world like a Catherine Wheel at Hallowe'en. Its landing was not as graceful as its take-off.

Thwack! It smacked into the cheek of the apprentice. He tasted blood on his lips, and his last words before he fainted in a heap were,

'It's got me.'

At this point the foreman came running out of the workshop, ranting and raving and wanting to know why nobody was at their work. The crowd melted away.

Jimmy got an official, written reprimand for the first time in an unblemished career. As for his apprentice – he was sent home in an ambulance and got a day off work without pay.

Workshop at Castle Espie

This was a very inspiring day and the weather was perfect. We were shown into a room with a view – and what a view!

I immediately felt very welcome as I settled at a long table and noticed tea and coffee and freshly-made scones laid on for us.

My first inspiration for a poem was when Noel had to go home with acute toothache. This unsettled me a little because I knew that he had been looking forward so much to the day.

Our visiting tutor was Martin Mooney and he soon had our noses to the grindstone while picking up valuable points at the same time.

After lunch we went outside to draft some ideas for an article or poem. The surprising thing was that although we all saw the same view and surroundings we all wrote quite differently.

I thought this was very good – because what a dull world it would be if we all thought and wrote alike.

Jean Galway

Stage Fright

So many entered with me
(say….stage right)
now gone
exit stage left and out of sight.

Yet here we are
acting quite well (so far)
hearts beating,
still eating
heartily…

Pirouetting,
sometimes jetting
to foreign parts.

Often we miss our lines,
we dry…..
life's prompter gives our cue
so with a sigh
we find our words again,
perform another day,
our comic act regain.

Some say,
"You look so well,"
so let's not dwell
on final act – Act Three…
our exit….and the curtain down.

Rosemary Williamson

Words

As birds can wing o'er oceans wide,
so words can fly through time and tide
and carry honey sweet….or aloes,
building nests in human hearts
and bringing joy or pain.

Rosemary Williamson

Specsavers
by
Jean Hinds

I loved looking through mum's button box and was amazed at how many different kinds there were.   All colours, in glass and plastic and metal and wood.

I came across a pair of circular red plastic things without any holes and joined in the middle.

'What funny buttons', I thought and went to find my mother.

When I asked her what they were she said, 'Hen's glasses'.

I thought that she was pulling my leg.   How could any hen see through things like these?

That was precisely the point – to stop the hens in question from pecking each other.

I don't know where they are now, but just imagine going to the Antiques Road Show' with a pair of hen's glasses.

The mind boggles – or goggles!

They might be worth a fortune.

To Sleep

Visit me sleep, with enfolding peace.
Humours restorative, healer of sadness,
Small money's richness, restriction's liberty.
Impartial to class, common to all,
Shield from the pressure of life's stress,
Jibs, barbs, dull pain of frustration.
Transport me from this strife and tension;
My gratitude will be endless for this;
Soft benison of comfort, warm safe bed,
In silent bedroom, with curtains drawn.
Clean pillows under drooping head
With sweet smelling luxurious sheets.
Give weary body chance to rest, warm
Dreaming in slumber, I'll see stars.

Ray Heath

The Enlightened Soldier

Any country that sends its soldiers to war should at least abide by three principles.

- *Give them an honest assessment as to why they must go to fight.*
- *The proper resources and equipment to ensure they can do the job properly.*
- *The most important! In the event of their death or return home badly wounded, they and their dependants will receive the best care and assistance available.*

Our soldiers in Iraq and Afghanistan have been badly let down on all three principles by our leaders. I am sure many serving in these hostile lands wonder why they are there. This poem might reflect their thoughts.

We looked around this hostile land
Hoping to liberate and bring the peace.
Like my comrades, I believed the spin.
Then, no one would believe,
The situation we are now in.
For many reasons,
Disillusionment is to the fore,
Comrades killed and wounded,
With civilians many, many more.
Long hours and hostility,
Never knowing friend from foe,
Ambushed, attacked,
Not knowing which way to go.

Our moral courage to focus
On dangers while we're there,
Comes from our training
And our ability to care.
In looking after one another,
We take enormous pride.
As a committed army,
With absolutely nothing to hide.

Pension worried army top brass,
Are paraded on display.
To tell a sceptic public,
Things have to be this way.
Ministers go on camera,
Sweat and gesticulate with hands,
While others strike wooden balls,
On manicured public lands.

The spin is over,
The top wobbles about to fall.
We don't believe them,
Yet must obey, every time they call.
Ministers and spin doctors,
Try to whip the top back up to speed.
But the spin cannot work again,
We will never pay it heed.

Things will get no different,
No end is in sight.
With prayers and good wishes,
We might get home alright.
No one wants to return alone.
Met by grieving relatives at the plane.
Our hope is to return en bloc,
And embrace our loved ones once again.

Tom Jamison

Waves

Special memories of idyllic days
walking and resting and enjoying the show
of sand-dunes and pebbles and pieces of driftwood
leading our gaze to the ebb and the flow.

The only real movement is the lapping of water
with gentle waves breaking like pearls swinging on strands
from a distant horizon through small rippling movements
and dispersing like magic on silvery sands.

The hills in the distance are dark but not threatening
a calming dimension over-arching the fair
beauty of nature and making a framework
to both link and divide the water and air.

The sky's a rare blue for this part of the country
and the cotton wool clouds have a shadowy sheen
as they flit from our feet over water and mountains
weaving the patterns of this special scene.

Gerry Miller

The Healer
by
William Fitzell

Danielle and Gregory Turner's marriage was in trouble; their relationship was beginning to unravel. They would trade insults at the drop of a hat, often over trivial matters. Never hanging around to discover he was in the wrong, Gregory Turner would grab his coat in a rage, hurl some obscenity over his shoulder at his wife, stamp out the house slamming the door behind him and head for the pub, leaving her in tears. Their children, Robert and Shelby tried not to get caught up in their parents' running battles. Robert's school work suffered while Shelby had turned into a weepy frightened little girl. Their mother and father were so wrapped up in their problems they habitually neglected their children. The marriage was on a downward spiral heading towards inevitable break-up.

The warring couple, realizing Christmas was close and not wanting to lose face with the neighbours, knew they would have to bury the hatchet if they were to get through the festive season like civilized people. They had promised the children they could have a pup. Though his heart was not in it, Gregory Turner kept his word and the family got in the car and headed for a farm on the western slopes of Slemish mountain, near Broughshane, to collect a pup, eight weeks old, and ready to leave its mother.

As soon as they got home they placed the pup in the middle of the room while they sat round and watched, not knowing what would happen next. With her fluffy white coat and her friendly wide open eyes and oversized paws she looked gorgeous. She recognized instinctively the leader of the pack as she toddled across the room to the father and rolled over in the submisive pose in front of him, as if to say 'You are the man.' Then sitting in front of him, and with great deliberation, the pup slapped a big paw in the air, inviting him to take it. Gregory Turner was impressed and a broad smile slowly crept across his face. The pup then turned to the others, and Mum, Robert and Shelby began to laugh and applaud as she danced around them with such delight, touching them with a soft wet nose, that said; 'Now I know you.' They laughed and Gregory Turner joined in their laughter, the laughter of joy. The pup had bonded with the family.

"What are we going to call her?" asked Mum .

"Let's name her after a celebrity," suggested Robert.

"It had to be a girl," Shelby moaned, "I wanted Barney. Can we call her Barney, mum?"

"Barney is a boy's name Shelby, you know that."

"We should try and come up with an original name," their father suggested.

The whole family talked among themselves but couldn't agree on a name. Then Robert had a bright idea. "Mum picked our names, I think she should pick a name for the pup; let's leave the choice with her." All eyes now turned to Danielle. Their mother thought for a moment, then, very quietly she said, "We'll call her Healer"

They agreed, and a Healer she became.

Topaz – My Cat

No music half so soothing
As your deep melodious purr,
No fabric half so silky
As your thick, soft Persian fur,

No human eyes so lovely
As your lustrous topaz glow.
O, is it any wonder puss
That I have loved you so?

The friendly little rubs and licks
With which you show affection.
I know no other pussy-cat
Could rise to your perfection.

But as I dug your little grave
Beneath the lilac tree
I thought by transmutation
I could keep you close to me.

The pleasure of delightful scent
And blossom edged with blue,
Brings me a measure of content
And turns my thoughts to you.

Eirene Armstrong

A Tale about Betty Jones: The Closet
by
Hannah Penton

Darkness. That's all I see. There is no sound. Just silence, apart from my rapid breathing. My heart beats fast, my hands are shaking and my teeth are chattering as if they would never stop. When will this nightmare end?
"HELP!" I shout, "Let me out. Please, let me out!"
I bang against the door, putting all my weight into it.
They always do this. They are like animals feeding off my fear and humiliation. They rule the school with such imposing dominance that no one dares stand up to them. It is hard to think of them as seventeen-year-old kids.
I'm not a genius. I get average grades, and don't wear braces or glasses, so I know for I fact that I'm not a nerd. I love art, which is really the only subject I excel at. I guess I use it as an outlet to the feelings that build up inside me. Most of the time I feel invisible, except when I'm with my friends, though they never get singled out like I do. It's always me.
"Poor insignificant Betty," I hear them call from the other side of the door, "Who's going to help you now?"
I bite my lip to stop from sobbing aloud. Tears stream down my face, and I shut my eyes even tighter. Perhaps if I imagine that I am in another place, like my room, this fear that is making me feel sick will go away.
I try it. It just makes me feel worse.
It's my fourth time here.
Locked in this darkness, with no way out. The feeling that any minute the walls around me are going to close in. Suddenly I spring up, letting panic take over rational thought. I no longer care what they think, only that I have to get out of here as fast as I can.
"LET ME OUT!" I scream, "I'll do anything. Please, just let me out!"
I am now shaking so bad that I have to sit down again. Sobbing, I continue my pleas, but to no effect.
A faint ring of laughter drifts under the door, and then the sound of footsteps fading away.
I am alone. Who will help me now?

Epiphany

I picked a yellow rose on Christmas Day,
the last.......it stood so solitary there
wearing a sparkling diadem of snow,
diffusing soft its radiance in the air.

If I should go and offer up a gift,
I cannot think that I should be so bold,
I wouldn't have the frankincense or myrrh,
but here upon my palm...so soft, so cold,
I had the gold.

Rosemary Williamson

Easter

Tell me the things
that give you joy
unsought,
not bought,
that made you think
you'd heard an angel sing,
and touched its feathered wing,
and I will know
how rich you are.

Rapiers of light
slicing through a day
that promised nothing much,
the prospect grey,
making it gold and bright
with their light.

Things that sometimes follow
after sorrow,
messages to say
don't grieve
don't leave your faith
for there is resurrection.

Rosemary Williamson

The Winner
by
Noel Spence

The last twist of the knife, a fourth goal conceded right on the final whistle. Jake watched his team troop disconsolately off the pitch, and then joined the handful of regulars shuffling into the Club Room. It struck him, as it did every Saturday, that while he was sunk in frustration and disappointment at yet another defeat, the other supporters were already exchanging the ritual after-match banter and wisecracks. Win or lose, the result seemed to make no difference to them.

In this, if in nothing else, Jake envied them. He knew he could never accept defeat with that kind of indifference. No, Jake was a brooder, a bad loser. What kind of a winner he might be was still undetermined. Only a few weeks away from the big Four O, and there was nothing, absolutely nothing, in all those years that he could look back on as a success, let alone a triumph.

As his Guinness swirled muddily into its glass behind the bar counter, Jake felt familiar black thoughts clouding into his head and darkening his mind. They oppressed him now on a daily basis, like a heavy mass, crouching over every part of his being, past and present, and obscuring any faint glimmer of hope for the days ahead.

He mechanically lowered his drink a few inches and stared into its thick darkness. As he raised the glass for a second swig, he caught his reflection in the mirror on the back wall behind the bar optics and glass shelving. Where once he might have seen a young man with dreams of love, wealth, happiness, there now squatted a loser, a man in a loveless marriage, in debt, in a dead-end job, in a rented house, in middling health, in middle age, and in the club room of a team that hadn't won a match since early September.

Add to this record last month's diabetes diagnosis, the recent row at work that had lost him the only friend he had, and a profoundly deaf son who lived away all week in a Special School, and there was Jake Duddy's scoresheet to date, as well as a forecast of results to come.

Jake joylessly finished his pint, thought about another one, nodded to the group watching the over-coloured race meeting on the large screen TV, and pushed out into the rawness of a December late afternoon.

His mind scanned ahead: he hoped Madge would be in the kitchen when he got back. He would go straight into the front room for the results, and avoid having to speak to her. The sound of her voice was now enough to set his nerves on edge.

There had been a time when she would joke that she knew the match result by the look on his face, but there were no jokes between them now, and it wasn't because his team could be depended on to lose every week. In any case, even if by some miracle they were to win a match, Jake doubted if his face could now assume any expression other than its regular fixed scowl. It was true what he had overheard said about him one week

in the club: "Jake looks as if he's always facing into the wind."
Madge. He couldn't shake her loose from his thoughts. The numbing truth was that he found her repulsive, he could hardly bear to look at her, let alone touch her. Her psoriasis had flared up again, worse than ever, covering her scalp as well as her arms and hands and legs. Also back was the recurrent cold sore on her lower lip that left her mouth pink and puffy, like a lump of well used bubblegum. A tiny little voice told Jake that he should be feeling sympathy for Madge, but all he could honestly recognise in himself were feelings of disgust and revulsion.

It was something else on the domestic front, however, that troubled him far more deeply than his thoughts about Madge. It concerned his son. Whenever Jonny came home at the weekends from the School, sometimes bringing a friend or two to stay over, he was always alive with the things they had done, the places they had been, the people they had met. So much was done for the students: there seemed to be a continuous round of outings, dances, concerts, parties, visits, sports. As Jake absorbed the exciting social life his eighteen year old son was enjoying, any parental feelings of pride and pleasure were swept over by a dark tide of envy and resentment. Appalling it might be, unnatural, unforgivable, but Jake was jealous of his own handicapped son.... He shuddered and tightened his scarf round his face as the cold wind sliced between the stark rows of houses, and the streetlights came flickering on.

Madge was steadily ironing in the kitchen. She heard Jake come in, and the TV go on. She sighed aloud, a habit she had developed. Jonny wasn't coming home this weekend. He was going to Aviemore for skiing lessons. Madge looked forward all week to his return at the weekends. Jonny was the one good thing in her life. All her love, her soft feelings, she gave to him. He deserved them. He was such a good-hearted, sweet-tempered boy. It was as though nature had in this way compensated him for his disability.

Madge smiled as she folded the clothes, even though she knew there would be no relief this weekend from her husband's cold, relentless bitterness. At least she had one breath of happiness in the smothering gloom of her marriage.

She was just finishing the last shirt when, without warning, the door burst open and Jake was there right in front of her. Madge knew at once that something was wrong, terribly wrong. He was standing looking right at her, and he was smiling. No, worse than that, more terrifying, he was making the half-choked guffawing sounds that she remembered from way back as her husband's form of laughing. Something else was wrong. His posture. The beaten man's hunch was gone, he was standing upright.

"Jake, what's wrong? What is it? Are you OK?"

Madge's belief that he had suffered some kind of brainstorm was confirmed the next moment when he said, "Madge," before clamping his hand over his mouth to imprison another guffaw. Jake hadn't called her by name for two years or more. Next thing, to the accompaniment of strangled chortlings, he took her by the hands across the ironing table. All doubt was gone, he had definitely flipped.

She was wondering whether to phone the doctor or run next door for help, when he burst out in a kind of sob,"Madge, Madge, I've done it. I can't believe it, I've done it. I've hit the big one. You're not going to believe this. I've won the pools. We're rich. Twenty three points, Madge, twenty three points, the big one, seven score draws and a no score, and I've got the lot. Madge, Madge, d'you know what this means, twenty three, seven threes and a two, the big one. Claims required for twenty three points. Dividend forecast excellent."

Drunk with joy, Jake repeated the winning formula several more times, adding details of complicated lines and perms that meant nothing to her, and were more of an attempt to confirm for himself the reality of his success. Abruptly he glanced at his watch and ushered Madge into the front room in time to catch the results on the other channel. His hands were trembling as he checked the numbers against his copy coupon, shouting 'Yes' with each draw, and making doubly sure by matching them again with the list of draws shown at the end of the results broadcast. There was no doubt about it, Jake had scooped the jackpot.

Excitement coursed through him like an electric current. "I told you, Madge, I told you, I always said I'd win the big one." Caught up in the euphoria, she didn't point out his lament every Saturday afternoon as he tossed the coupon in a ball into the fire: No chance. What's the use? Waste of time. Me win anything? I'm a born loser, a beaten docket.

Jake didn't know yet how much he had won, or if there were any other winners, but he was certain that it was a matter of hundreds of thousands, possibly a million or more. He kept sitting down and getting up again, talking non-stop, and at moments seemed almost on the verge of tears. The win and its ramifications liberated a frenzy of mixed thoughts and feelings in him. As well as the obvious satisfaction of telling that little poisonous Welsh git of a boss what he could do with his job, and the delirious visions of new car, big house, and similar material possessions, Jake discovered gentler fancies stealing into his mind, the kind of considerations he hadn't entertained in years. Among them were the most expensive treatments for poor Madge's skin disease, and the best private specialists to examine Jonny's hearing condition. How can money be the root of all evil when it can kindle such worthy intentions....

Jostling for space too, however, were darker notions. Jake regretted having ticked the No Publicity box, but he'd make sure just the same that everybody knew of his glorious win. There were a few in particular whose faces he'd love to see when they heard Jake Duddy had won a million or more.

Derek Gooding! Derek Gooding! Yes, yes, yes, Derek Gooding. Jake had hated him all the way up through school, especially when Gooding had gone on to university and higher things.

That little moment a few months back jagged him again. Jake had been downtown and had chanced to look into the smart restaurant beside his bus stop. There in his flash suit, and in the company of a stunning young woman, sat Gooding, his dark red wine glass raised, his laundered white plumage glowing in the candlelight. He looked up and must have seen Jake because there was a self-satisfied smirk on his face. Jake shuddered now in anticipation as he envisaged Gooding's response to the news of his big win……

Tender sentiments returned as he watched Madge fold away the eternal ironing board. He rose to a joke. "Madge, it's the end of the Iron Age, it's the Golden Age now for the Duddy family."

Madge looked up with tears in her eyes, her poor face strangely pretty behind the reddish patches. "It's scary. What happens now?"

What happens now? How many times he had fantasised about precisely that. He did so again, only this time it was no fantasy, it was for real. Another spasm of excitement quivered right through him, and he snorted through his nose in his efforts to subdue a triumphant laugh.

He spread his copy coupon on the telephone table in the hall, took a deep breath, and with a hand that shook a little in spite of his best efforts, dialled the familiar number.

"Littlewoods Pools Office. May I help you?"

"Yes, I've got twenty three points on this week's coupon." Jake's voice was controlled, apart from the slight tremor when he got to the second syllable of the last word.

"Thank you, sir. Could I have your name and address, your reference number, which you'll find in a little box at the bottom of your coupon, and the Agency reference, if there is one filled in on the coupon."

Jake gave her the information, aware of the contrast between her level professional tone and his own unsteady delivery. He tried a wink to Madge, who was cowering in the corner as though afraid of the enormity and speed of events.

"Thank you. Just hold the line for a moment and I'll be right back to you."

Most people have at least one defining moment in their lives, an instant that shapes or colours the remainder of their existence, or their perception of it. For Jake Duddy that moment was expressed in nine flat words that reached him next down a telephone line:

"We are not in receipt of your coupon, sir."

For a second the import of the words was delayed, but when it struck the effect was the same as if Jake had jumped into a pool of ice cold water. His breath was sucked out of him, his stomach was a vacuum, his legs were rubber. How he managed to articulate a reply he could never have explained.

"But you must have got it. I posted it myself, first class, on Thursday morning."

"There's no mistake on our part, sir. Our system guarantees that."

Jake spluttered some irrelevant details about exactly how and where and when he had posted his coupon, but the woman was totally confident that it had not been received. She had the manner of someone trained to deal with drunks, cranks, losers.

"We'll check it again if you wish, sir," she finished, "and call you back if anything shows up." Her tone said that nothing was going to show up. Jake's head was a whirlpool of bewilderment, disappointment, rage. He kept repeating, again and again, "There must be some mistake. I posted it myself on Thursday morning. I posted it myself, out at New Meadows. I dashed through the rain and posted it myself. They must have got it. There must be some mistake."

But there was no mistake. Jake controlled his rising despair and trembling hands enough to ring back, and was informed by a different woman, "There are no jackpot winners this week."

It was true. All his dreams were gone, his big moment was in ruins. But why? How? He had definitely posted the coupon first thing on Thursday morning on his way to work. In confusion, in bitter self-pity and wretchedness of mind, Jake felt his head was going to explode. It used to be when he was drunk and everything was whirling he could close his eyes and wait for the dizziness to decrease, but this was worse, a hundred times worse. Instead of reducing, the terrible giddiness was intensifying until he really felt his brain was going to burst.

Madge was sobbing steadily in the corner, perhaps in sympathy for him or for herself, or from a more general sorrow, but Jake wasn't even aware of her presence. How long he had waited for some kind of success, some stroke of good fortune, and now to have it cruelly torn away from him. And what were the odds of a repeat, a second chance: if it was about a million to one hitting the jackpot once, the odds against Jake filling again were astronomical, incalculable. He might as well pack in the whole thing. Why had he believed for a moment that luck had smiled on him, when the evidence of his entire life marked him out as a no-hoper.

Just at the point when he felt the boiler of his mind was about to blow, an emergency valve mercifully opened to release the bursting pressure. The Post Office! That's where the fault lay, with the Post Office. That's who had robbed him of everything, that's where he would find his target. The blessed relief of rage. It didn't reduce the pounding in his head, but it redirected its force into a savagery against the public service that had left his hopes in ruins.

Jake was at the head of the small queue outside the main post office on Monday morning. His headache was that of a man who hadn't slept for two nights and who doubted if he would ever enjoy a peaceful night's sleep in his life again, but there was now a focus and desperate determination that kept his inner tumult under control.

By a tremendous effort of will Jake suppressed his anger sufficiently to explain to the woman behind the counter what had happened. With her wrenched -back hair and prominent front teeth, she looked for all the world like Bugs Bunny. She listened carelessly to Jake's accusations, unimpressed by the enormity of the delivery failure and its consequences for the sender. This was not what she wanted from her first customer first thing on a Monday morning.

When Jake had finished his arraignment of the entire Post Office system, the woman wrinkled her nose, and started to 'rabbit' on about first and second deliveries, and compensation up to £30 and £500. What was the stupid bitch talking about, hadn't she heard that he had lost a million pounds or more by the negligence of her organisation?

"So," the recital finished, "if you didn't send it Recorded Delivery or Registered Post, all we can do is put a trace on it."

Jake was spluttering with impatience and frustration. "Is putting it in the box not good enough any more? Is the Post Office not responsible for looking after and delivering people's mail? Is New Meadows some kinda backwoods, or something?"

The rabbit stiffened. "New Meadows? I'm sorry, sir, but if you posted your item in our New Meadows sub branch, you'll have to make your enquiry there. The trace will have to be put on from there." Her tone said that her part in the case was now terminated.

Jake wanted to throttle and possibly skin the creature, but he swallowed hard and told her how he had posted his coupon in a post box, not in the sub post office.

"Post Box? What Post Box? There is no post box at New Meadows, and I should know, sir, for I happen to live at New Meadows, and have done for thirty years. I'm sorry, sir, but you're mistaken. Next."

Jake's protestations were to no avail, and he stumbled home in a fury so strong that it almost supplanted his distress at having lost a fortune. He dragged Madge into the car. "No post box, no post box? She'll need to do better than that before I'm finished with her. Does she know who she's dealing with?"

The tirade continued all the way out to New Meadows, Madge crouched in the back seat in silent misery. Jake finally pulled up in front of a bright red Post Office box sunk in a newly-built curved brick wall.

Even as he was pointing it out to Madge, Jake realised his mistake. There was no lettering on the postbox, no times of collection, no public information. What he was looking at, what he had entrusted his precious coupon to, was a household letter box set into a private garden wall.

A sickness overwhelmed him at the moment of discovery, and another army of terrible thoughts started to batter his beleagured brain.

"That's not a post box, Jake," came a small voice from the back. "That's somebody's letter box. Look, there's a big GR in gold. It's an antique one. I'm surprised you didn't notice that."

It was the closest Madge would come to blaming him outright, but Jake noticed a hint of satisfaction in her voice. The truth reached him in that instant.. Madge hated him. His wife hated him. In his despair Jake almost welcomed the revelation, like a man cast down beyond hope perversely invites the pain of further misfortune.

If only he had left things as they were. Jake used to leave his coupon each week with the shopkeeper on the corner who acted as a pools Agent, but when the shop was robbed a few months earlier and cleared of most of its stock, Jake decided it was too risky to continue the practice, and started sending off the coupons himself. If only, if only. And now who could he blame but himself. He was utterly alone in his suffering, nobody cared, not even his family, and it was all down to his own mistake. Yes, it had been raining and he had raced from the car and thrust the envelope into the box, and it was, after all, a post box originally, but the fault still lay with him.

"It's not fair," he cried out loud with the helpless passion of a child, " how was I to know the difference? They shouldn't allow these things to be used as letter boxes. And look at me, look what's happened to me."

Jake was almost in tears, at the bottom of the pit, when suddenly, for the second time, in the midst of his desperate grief, the lifeline of anger was thrown to him. Of course, of course! Why hadn't the bastard who owned the letter box not posted his coupon on!

That's what should have happened. If he had had any decency at all, he should have posted it on. Jake didn't stop to ask himself if he would have behaved decently in the same circumstances. No, his frantic mind was off and running on a new scent, the victim this time an easier one, an individual instead of a government body.

His reeling brain steadied. He had it. He would go home, get himself resettled, recharged, ready for battle, and next morning bright and early he would present himself at the door of the hated householder, and let justice take whatever form it chose…..

The cold winter sunlight slanted into the room and lit the sleeping man's pillow. It was enough to waken him. Although he had driven home dog-tired straight from the airport, he had slept badly, probably owing to a combination of jet-lag and mental activity.

Yes, it had been a hectic five-day visit to Boston, but a hugely successful one, and he was back with a diary stuffed with useful names, and a briefcase containing three actual black and white deals. What was it that wealthy old Bostonian had said to him: a contact is only one letter away from a contract. Neat.

He stretched and looked out of the bedroom window. The new driveway was a good job, and, apart from a couple of little thin patches, the lawn had taken well.

His next look was ahead. First a glass of orange juice, followed by a cup of the coffee he had brought home with him, and then a couple of lengths in the inside heated swimming pool. After that he'd need to go down and collect his mail at the Post Office. Oh yes, he'd check to make sure nobody had mistaken his private letterbox for the real thing, as had happened a few times just after the wall and pillars were finished; he had been quick to post the letters on immediately, not wishing to inconvenience any of his new neighbours.

Then before lunch the triumphant appearance at the office with the captures he'd made in the States. He could hardly wait. He stretched again, a stretch of satisfaction. Yes, life was good for Derek Gooding, a man at ease with himself and at peace with all the world…..

Portavogie Man
(Whither To Awa)

Whither away in the soft gleaming light
On the road that encircles the water
And the shore and the sky spawn the wild goose cry
Wi' the tower standing up on the palm of the land
Wi' the black rocks knuckling under.
Aye.   Whither away?

Whither away in the soft gloamin' hour
Down the road that runs roun' the water
An' the wild birds flock like the skirts of a girl
Cast in the wind to scallop and birl
An' the pull o' the night is all grey and gold
Where the whins are never done coddin' the cold
An the wife'll be coddlin'me
Awa' down the Airds tae the sea.

Aye. Whither awa' in the darkenin' licht
Doon the pad that follies the watter,
An' the starlin's blaw like the knots on a net
That's thrown fir the fish in the sea
An' Mac Mairdrie, ma dug, is snared on a bush
An' is greetin' her heid aff fir me
Awa' doun the Airds tae the sea.

At the set o' the day at the sea.

Dorothy Pyper

Above – some of the members at the 1-day workshop in Scrabo Tower
Below - some of the audience who attended the *Evening with Jennifer Johnston*

A Smug Cat
by
Jean Hinds

Taking my two dogs for a walk I passed a house in my neighbourhood
where a black cat lay basking on the path as if it had just been given a
saucer of cream.   Then I noticed something small and dark beside it. At
first I thought it was a stone or a small piece of wood.
Tying the dogs to the gate I went up and discovered that it was a young
thrush.
Cat looked at me and I looked at cat.
Bird just looked dazed.
I thought to myself, "Don't think that I am going to congratulate you on
your catch!"
As I moved closer the cat fled and I was able to pick up the fledgling. At
the same noticed I noticed a dead bird in the next driveway.
I picked them both up and stood wondering what I was going to do with a
live stunned bird, a dead bird and two dogs.
A tiny voice in my head said, "Don't interfere with nature".
Often when I am watching nature programmes on television I don't
understand why the camera men don't intervene even when some
beautiful animal is being mauled by a lion or other fierce beast.
But this was on my own doorstep and I didn't think that Mother Nature
would mind if I saved one little bird.
Just then a neighbour came out of one of the houses to see what I had and
kindly she took both of the birds into her care.
Thank goodness we are not camera women.
I never did find out whether the bird survived – maybe it is the one that
whistles at me some days as it sits on the neighbour's roof.
Or maybe it is whistling at the cat.
Anyway, I whistle back.

The Tap Dancers

Tap tap tapping is sounding on the pavement
tapping and laughing is coming down our way
we hear laughing and tapping in the distance
with all the promise of a happiness day.

The tap tap tapping sound is coming closer
and also the sound of laughter starts to swell
the tap tap tapping is a marching drumbeat
and is drawing our attention like a spell.

Suddenly three young men appear together
with one who's leading the rhythm of their walk
they saunter in a sort of dance formation
they're always tapping and laughing as they talk.

First we see the faces and then the bodies
captivating all the passers with the sound
everybody steps aside to let them by
with their white canes tapping smartly on the ground.

One of these three young men is fully sighted
and is telling to the others what they pass
one who is blind from birth is tapping strongly
and the one who's newly-blind is learning fast.

Tap tap tapping passes along the pavement
as they take a learning curve so very steep
with their walking and tapping always laughing
but when he's home again I wonder – does he weep?

Gerry Miller

Memories of a Country Road
by
Tom Jamison

I was brought up in a normal, suburban, working class environment, one generation removed from a rural farming background. My father and mother kept close ties with our rural past by regularly visiting relatives in the country. Especially my grandmother on my father's side.

My sister and I always found it magical when we all got off the bus and walked from the main road into the narrow winding country road on which she lived. Even my father who worked hard all week in the building trade seemed to have more of a spring in his step when his feet touched that road.

It was like entering another world. I am sure it rained sometimes, but from memory the sun always seemed to shine, giving life and energy to the fields and hedgerows. Wild flowers, especially primroses and violets adorned the banks and verges. Tall foxgloves grew proudly, each one trying to catch the eye as if by way of a greeting. From the hedgerows, a constant serenade, birds, all in practice for some great concert. Each in its season, the lonesome call of the cuckoo. From the hayfield the throaty rasp of the corncrake. The lark surveying all from high above.

Cows ambling home for milking, closely bunched, all different colours, no modern uniformity then. From the lark's high viewpoint they must have looked like a patchwork quilt wafting in the breeze.

But the pace of life moves everything onwards. The road so cherished, fades with the passage of time into a distant memory yet it is good to let one's thoughts occasionally travel back along the road. My sister who has lived abroad for many years and I did just that on one of our regular long distance telephone conversations. The country road of our childhood had not been mentioned by either of us for countless years, yet we were recalling it in detail.

Again I travel the road, drawn to it by these distant memories. The primroses, violets, foxgloves and other flowers gone, replaced by a film of tight dust that covers the verges and hedgerows. Probably caused by a combination of pesticides, chemicals, heavy machinery and vehicles. No song birds sing, the concert finished long ago. No cuckoo, corncrake or lark, only silence. Cows don't meander the road anymore, a quarry gouges rock out of their once gentle pastures. Farm houses, once a hive of activity, stand silent and empty, now owned by the quarry.

Disillusionment could come easily, but as the old saying goes, " You cannot stop progress." It is most important to remember, we were there. We walked, saw, touched, smelt and listened to that road at a time when nature really blessed it. Many people here or abroad will have similar memories of their childhood road. The important thing to remember is that good memories cannot be taken away from you. My sister agrees with this philosophy.

The Hooded Menace

Parkas and i-pods and crowded streets with the bustle of
rush-hour and the crawling fleets of taxis and buses that
transport home from office blocks the commuting hordes (who spend
half their lives travelling) from all the pressure where the mind
is numbed as business locks freedom together
with family life out of the frame

Queues that are growing look at watches and start to grumble
At delays in the transport caught in a complete jumble
with vans illegally parked (just for a moment!) that snare
up the system and frustrate the nerves already jangled
by lights and folk crossing in droves and street vendors and all
are inescapably trapped.

On an over-crowded bus with many people standing,
his hood over his head and his i-pod loudly blasting,
a youth is oblivious to the hordes that surround him
with his feet and his bag on the seat which is facing him.
His mind is blanked with something that blots out the old woman
standing painfully beside him.

A man taps him on the shoulder until he gives a look
with a glazed stare in his eyes that fellow travellers took
as a warning of danger to those who get in his way.
For a moment all is tied, imitating the slow motion
Of the traffic snarled outside, just watching and waiting for
something to happen.

He sees the crowding menace, jumps up and grabs his bag
and looks wildly with a grimace while others hold their breath and
anticipate some dangers as he reaches to the lady
with elegant slim fingers and helps her to sit down while
all his discomfort lingers. 'I am so very sorry.
Please forgive me my bad manners.'

Gerry Miller

"December Bride" by Sam Hanna Bell

This riveting and haunting novel richly deserves a first, second and third reading. "December Bride" can rival any novel of the twentieth century with its descriptively beautiful and stunning style. Every word counts and every word is the right word.

The countryside of the farming community around Strangford Lough plays a leading role in this novel. Sam Hanna Bell uses words – descriptive, alliterative and onomatopoeic – to such intense and evocative effect that it came as no surprise to me to learn that initially he was a painter and studied at the Belfast College of Art. We see a loved landscape through an artist's acutely observant eye.

The eternal and relentless themes of this novel compete for attention in the lives of its characters. Poverty - or the fear of it - is the prime motivator. The Great Famine is almost within living memory. Hard, laborious, all-weather work is the essential background to the lifestyle. Religion and Christian morals, for good or bad, vie with mysterious pagan influences. Politics provide an uneasy presence, caught up as they are with the didacts of the clergy and their religious utterances.

All the emotions created by a precarious and hard existence are present, including love, lust, avarice, compassion, hatred and envy. These feelings are heightened by the stimulation of religious and moral attitudes as well as by the effects of alchohol - thrift's old adversary.

I feel that the influences of both poetry and painting have contributed strongly to the writing of this book. I hear echoes of Thomas Hardy, William Wordsworth and Emily Bronte's 'Wuthering Heights'.

Also I am reminded of the later work of the painter John Turner, especially 'Slavers – slave ship throwing over the dead and dying – typhoon coming on' about which Simon Sharma (Power of Art, BBC tv, 17th November 2006) stated that Turner had 'reached his greatest match between message and form – payoff freedom'.

Sam Hanna Bell, writing in the 1940's about events occurring at the beginning of the twentieth century, surely had knowledge of these works. As a prelude to the novel he quotes Thomas Hardy – what portents are there, the excerpt from 'Honeymoon-Time at an Inn' asks, with the reply - 'tis the lot of all'. In this way Sam Hanna Bell emphasises the nature of the eternal truths of life which the story describes through the portrayal of the characters.

Sarah Gomartin is a wonderful, vital and engrossing heroine. She is mysterious, enigmatic and acts instinctively. I quote – 'some said that she was a mouse, others that she was a sly lady'. 'Sarah had an amazing capacity for hard work' 'She's a cold pale one, thought Frank, with no sport in her. Then he caught her calm ever-moving glance and felt uncertain again'.

The shipwreck of the rowing boat is pivotal in the narrative. Sarah 'felt a surge of kinship and love for her three companions. Her fear was subdued and lost in this feeling of kinship'.

Sarah is saved from drowning by the supreme sacrifice of the old farmer Andrew. This experience ties her emotionally to both his sons. The Rev. Sorleyson's reaction to Andrew's sacrifice alienates her from both him and the church he stands for.

Sarah is proud but cautious. Her manner is simple and direct. She becomes enmeshed in a love and a passion for both brothers. To Hamilton, the older and steadier brother, she 'felt full of remorse, and an urgent desire to please him'. Sarah can scarcely believe that men find her attractive – 'there's pain and evil in me now', she tells her mother. She is a penniless woman whose beauty stirs lust in the two brothers. Frank ensures that her one proper suitor, Pentland, feels that she is already involved with him.

Sarah is proud to have two men after years of humiliation. Her break from her mother fills her and Frank with 'remorse and anger'. Later, Sarah is pregnant and desperate to 'keep her own foot in the house' and neglects her mother. The realisation of Sarah's pregnancy results in her mother's fatal heart attack. With the birth of her son Sarah 'had never known contentment like this before'.

Sarah was tormented by a superstitious belief that 'some day she would have to pay for her actions'. Her morally lawless involvement with and love for Hamilton and Frank are starkly contrasted with the Rev. Sorleyson's cowardly, loveless and insincere marriage – 'bound for a lifelong duress to stifle the fruitless blaze of anger, and perform all the little acts that convention expected'.

The love between Sarah, Frank and Hamilton just barely survives the crushing forces of nature and religious convention.

The themes of sin, retribution and redemption pervade this beautiful and classic novel.

P. Heather Johnston

Forgotten Teddy

We lie here together, this box is now home.
Long forgotten, we feel completely alone
Full of hope I remain at the ready
But it's a sad end for a loving teddy.

How different it all was at the start.
I was new, things were perfect and fine.
Cherished and loved, I was the favourite one,
Life was so good at that time.

I know I am not the same as when new,
Some of my limbs are now askew.
One ear is missing, my fur rubbed thin,
But my eyes are bright and I still have my grin.

As the years rolled on, we all saw the change.
New toys arrived that we found very strange.
Batteries were needed to make them last,
We originals were destined to the past.

Our fate was decided one morning in Spring,
When the lady said," This house will be cleaned.
These toys will all go, or be put away."
Together we hoped to be allowed to stay.

We were all gathered up, two dollies and I,
With some cowboys and soldiers that belonged to the boy.
My fate in the balance, I waited to see,
Is it the dustbin or charity shop for me.

Then a voice that I recognised spoke loud and clear,
"These toys all must stay, I like the thought of them here."
A grown woman now, it was my little girl,
We were so excited we all gave a twirl.

So in this box we all have to stay,
Patiently waiting for a better day.
Our wish is that grand children will come along,
When they open this box we will burst into song.

Tom Jamison

The Goldfish

Within my globe of glass and H2O
Complete in a world, designed for life
Limited, but adequate for me.
As I swim round, indifferent to
That other world, beyond my own
Which only intervenes to cause disturbance
To the surface of my pool
When feeding me or tapping on the glass.
Since tepid water suits my style
And room service on constant call
Provides for needs limited indeed.
I swim and fan myself at ease
With outspread fins, my rounded mouth
Blows bubbles which rise to show
Which way is up and which is down.

Ray Heath

Kobe

Coloured cabbages, topiaried in concrete tubs.
My knees sliced by the freezing wind off the inland sea.
Bustling people, laughing.   Men in godowns
Open to the street, drinking warm sake,
Their strong slit eyes, bright in round faces
With grinning teeth.
Tramcars rattle by, air reeks of pungent fumes.
Entering Moto Mache, a Japanese woman bows
And steps aside. I bow back amazed,
At this picture from a teacup, quaint
In shimmering kimono.   In Moto Mache
West meets east, scotch whisky and cameras.
Men show films on a counter top, an old newsreel.
The fall of Singapore through Japanese eyes.
I watch privily, they noisy and jubilant.
Suddenly; sensing the intrusion, silence.
Embarrassed, they disperse, equipment stowed away
Perhaps to be shown on another day?
The assistant, prim in western suit, asks:
'May I serve you, sir?'

Ray Heath

Tunnel Vision
by
Eddie Whiteside

I pretended the jibes didn't hurt, but they did. Being called 'chicken', and having this derisive name accompanied by squawking noises and the flapping of elbows in imitation wings, was enough to make any ten year old flinch.

My two mockers were my brother and cousin, both a year younger than me, and the source of their scorn was my refusal to accept their dare to walk back through the tunnel with them.

No appeal of mine about the stupidity and danger of the challenge carried any weight. For them it would be fun; it would be exciting, and nobody was going to dissuade them from their adventure. I watched the darkness swallow them up as they went into the tunnel, then ran round, with trepidation, to wait for them at the other end.

Back in those long-ago days of the 1950's, before package holidays abroad, we were usually bundled off to my auntie's near Whitehead for the summer holidays.

Her little cottage, at the foot of the cliff, was a short distance from the shore, access to which only required crossing over the double-track railway lines - not a difficult task as the security fence was just waist high, and consisted of three parallel wires attached to some wooden posts.

A few yards from our usual crossing point was the tunnel – a black mouth carved into the rocky overhang - menacing yet inviting.

I had taken up my agreed position for only a minute or so when I saw the smoke. It was the Belfast train in the distance, rushing at great speed towards me.

Instantly an avalanche of panic overwhelmed me. I imagined the impending carnage in the tunnel, and the vision terrified me. My whole body started to shake and whimpering noises were coming from my throat. Hardly able to breathe or see through the blinding tears, I struggled to think of what to do. I found myself stumbling to the tunnel entrance. Standing in the middle of the track, I cupped my hands and yelled as hard as I could.

'There's a train coming. There's a train coming.'

My voice seemed to rumble down the shaft, reverberating off the walls in a muffled, indistinct echo. I continued shouting as long as I dared. A warning whistle came from the train and the ground started to shake beneath my feet. I staggered out of its way and saw it hurtle into the tunnel, snorting like an angry, devouring beast and spewing acrid smoke all around me. I collapsed over the fence and vomited. By this time I was sobbing uncontrollably.

'There's the big chicken over there,' said my brother.

Sweet relief flooded me, his voice instant healing. I managed to blurt out between racking sobs, 'What happened?'

'Some oul fella yelled at us in the tunnel,' my cousin said. 'Roared something about a train coming so we ran. Lucky you weren't there.' He started the clucking hen noises again. One part of me wanted to hug him, another to punch him in the mouth. But the whole experience had drained from me all capacity for any physical activity. I said nothing then and to this day have remained silent.

Villanelle
(using the bones of Dylan Thomas)

Brightness approaching heralds the end of night.
Rising I force myself towards the day
Seeing the features of my room flooded by light.

Though every item I can see is right
The greyness creates a softness, when they
Were formerly invisible in dark of night.

They solidify to hardness in the bright.
As day advances washing into every bay,
Splashing the room, every wall with light.

Darkness now completely put to flight.
So that I see before me a clear way
Leading me into day and out of night.

With day, all features become real to sight
Where before gloom reigned now all is gay
With colour, shade and texture in day's light.

Thus the day produces images of height,
Proportion and depth, which we pray;
Existed in the gloom and darkness of night.
Now clearly visible, exposed in the light.

Ray Heath

The Harvest
by
Jean Galway

One harvest day I was admiring a lovely field of golden grain, when I heard the approaching sound of the combine-harvester. In a few minutes it was manoeuvred into a field through an opening almost too narrow for its size, followed by two tractors each equipped with trailers to collect the grain. In the space of about half an hour, the grain was safely gathered in with only the straw left for the bailer to make into bales which always remind me of giant portions of shredded wheat. This set me thinking of what we call 'the good old days?' and I leave you to decide which were the good old days, then or now?

Seventy years earlier the harvest was a much more lengthy procedure. First a man would scythe and tie the grain around the gate. This left an opening for the horse-drawn reaper to drive straight to the sward, without trampling any grain. Tidiness was very important. The reaper had two seats, one for the driver of the horse and the other for the man who oversaw that the cut grain was lying in a good position for the man or woman to tie into bundles, which were called sheaves. Very often a yelp of pain and maybe an occasional oath could be heard as a thistle came into contact with someone's hand. After the sheaves had been tied, they were stooked, that is set upright with the stubble side downwards, four to six sheaves in a stook, one propping the other up. They were then left there to dry out before being carted home to the stack-yard to be built into stacks. With the fields cleared of crops, it was an extra place to walk or play. The ditches were full of wild flowers, such as meadow-sweet, knapweed, purple vetch and corn marigold. I feel that with so much spraying with pesticides, our flora is getting very rare indeed, but I bet the person who got jagged with that big thistle wouldn't have minded if it had got a lethal dose several weeks before!!

On a dry day after the stooks had dried out, they were transported by horse and cart into the stack-yard. The bases had been built previously, either round or oblong, whatever the farmer preferred. These bases consisted of big stones covered with briars and whins. The idea was to build the stacks on these bases in order to let a certain amount of air circulate, otherwise they would have overheated and been useless. The last chore was to thatch the stacks to keep them dry until the thresher arrived. In the meantime the stack-yard made a great play area, with all its nooks and crannies, perfect for all kinds of games. Remember, we had to make our own entertainment. We didn't have electricity so there was no television or computers, but what we never had we didn't miss.

What excitement when the day was set for the thresher to come! The day before its arrival my Mother did a big baking of soda, wheaten and treacle farls, pancakes, fruit soda-bread and apple tarts. My Father would be away rounding up the neighbours to help. It was the custom for each farmer to help the other and to bring their workmen with them. Usually the thresher came in the evening. The driver and his helper would fill the boiler with water, then stoke up the fire under it with coal. This was to boil the water and so create steam to drive the mill. This meant it was easier to get steam up for an early start in the morning. Two men would be on the stack forking sheaves down to the platform of the thresher. Two more would be opening the sheaves and passing them to be spread out and fed in to the mill. Two more men would be on the shute, where they put the good grain into hessian sacks. The chaff fell on the ground, where most of it was waste, but sometimes was used to fill or refill mattresses. My husband told the story of a wee boy who had been absent from school the previous day and when the teacher asked the reason for his absence the boy said, "Please Miss, I was away getting chaff for the bed." The poor woman didn't know what he was talking about, but the rest of the class did and had a good laugh. I'm sure the teacher was wondering why chaff was needed for the bed.

At mid-day the men had dinner. A big pot of potatoes would be boiled to eat with the soup and meat, followed by all the goodies mother had baked the day before, washed down with plenty of tea or, if anyone preferred it, sweet milk or buttermilk. This was a social occasion and work was forgotten for a brief time.

The work had restarted as we raced home from school, anxious not to miss the final hours of the thresher.

I can still picture the scene so vividly, the men with the bottoms of their trousers tied with binder string, their faces streaked with grime and sweat, and most of them armed with pitch forks. Nearby was our terrier dog waiting for mice or rats. They usually made their nests at the bottom of the stacks and would wait until the last sheaf was lifted before trying to escape. I made a quick dash into the house, after all I had no trousers to tie the bottoms, only a pair of bare legs and I was terrified of mice and rats. Soon the thresher was on its way, having made sure there was plenty of fuel to take them to the next farm – its work complete for another year.

The Chief Witness
by
Eirene Armstrong

(by himself)

Thanks Bert. A whiskey for me. No water. I don't like it 'dulterated. And that's my lot for tonight. I daren't come home a wee bit over the limit two nights runnin'. The police saved me last night but I'll be on me own tonight. Got to be in by half-eleven. If I can't make it in time I may immigrant.

I'll tell you the first bit again, for Bert here missed the start. You know the good time we had here last night. Well I reckons on account of the celebrations I can risk leavin' a bit later. Could've got a taxi but I thinks half a mile isn't that much. I could walk it and walk off some of the booze. I wasn't all that steady on my feet what with the dark and that. I had to jump smartlike into the hedge when I hears the car. Would have hit me if I hadn't been quick. Well, I picks meself up and knows right away something is afoot. No lights, ye see. I sez, Andy, I sez, they're up to no good drivin without lights. Well, they passes me and slows a bit. I sees it's more like a van than a car. Then it stops and the back opens up. They pushes something out and away they goes. Top speed. Dumpin', I thinks. At Quarry Lane. You know the bother there's been over that. My Maggie's been leadin' the protest meetings about the filth, rats an' all. Illegal it is. But the police don't bother. If it was drunks now they'd bother, or catchin' you drivin'. Thon quarry's full and it's dumpin' along the lane they're at now. I hurries up and sees it's a heap of old clothes lyin' at the side of the road. Didn't even bother to throw it into the lane. I gives it a bit of a kick over an' then I near collapses. It's a body. A young fella. White face you see. I sobers up quick. I was able to run to that house up the road. I bangs on the door but they wouldn't open. No neighbourliness nowadays. Won't help people even in emergencies but I knows I have to get the police, so I keeps on knockin' an' kickin' an' shoutin' about the body. If you don't stop that, they sez, there'll be another body. I didn't stop. I done my duty. They rang the police in the the end. I mus' say they were no time in comin'.

Well, just a half. Thanks, Alec. Cheers!

Nice man the inspector. Very respectful to me. Course he knew I was vital to the 'vestigation. A big crowd o' them in no time. White suits. Put up a tent. Strung tapes all round. I tells the inspector the young lad was flung from a van. Probably got a bad knock on the head. But the pathlogist man said he was dead afore the fall. It was a knife in his back what done for him. Public kept away, but not me. Chief witness you see. In the middle of it all I thinks Maggie'll kill me, so I asks the inspector for his phone – you know, the type that all the kids have nowadays. He dials for me and I 'splain to Maggie. I tell her I'm chief witness in an accident but I'm not hurt nor nothin'. Pity, says she, an' slams the phone down. The inspector sees I'm for it when I get home an' bein' thankful to me for all the help he gets me into a patrol car an' takes me home.   I 'Splains it all to Maggie so she knows I'm tellin' no lies. Never believes a word I say, that woman.

Well durin' the ride home I was able to give the inspector a few pointers. It's gang warfare, I tells him. Somebody's tryin' to muscle in on somebody else's patch. So they cancels him. The drug boys don't stand for anybody else tryin' to take over. The kid was prob'ly informin' on them so they had to deal with him. Don't know what they're lettin' theirselves in for when they tangle with the drug boys. Anyway, as I sez, I was a great help. Prob'ly be chief witness in court. Had a newspaper man round this mornin', but I'm no pushover. I draws meself up and sez I can't divulge important information until they give me police clearance. Then he bungs me a tenner.

So drink up boys. This round's on me.

One Stormy Night
by
Jean Hinds

Spring was on its way. You could tell from the tiny buds forming on the trees, the bulbs pushing up through the soil and the birds pairing up and househunting.

A pair of bluetits chose a nesting box on our garage wall and began to carry material for the nest. In due course the hen laid six eggs. The dad bird fed the mum while she sat on the nest to keep the eggs warm until one by one they hatched out. Then the parents were kept busy flying in and out in search of food. As soon as one arrived with a full beak the other set off – no delivery service in their world.

Then one night a fierce storm arose and in the morning the box was lying on the ground. I thought that the birds must all be dead, but to my joy the parents kept flying out and returning with food for the family.

The box was replaced more securely on the wall and on the next Sunday morning, at eight o'clock precisely, out of the small entrance hole appeared the head of the first chick, followed by a thin little body – and then it flew the short distance across to the wall where a parent was waiting.

It was followed by number 2, number 3, and number 4. Number 5 peeped out and decided to stay where it was. While all this was happening the mother bird was still feeding them. Number 5 was the last, and eventually it ventured out and reluctantly flew across to join the rest of its family.

The mother bird then cleaned out the nest although one egg which had not hatched was left – I suppose five chicks were enough to rear at one time. Later in the day, after some trial flights from wall to wall they all disappeared.

I felt sad and experienced a sense of loss, but later in the day all seven flew back and lined up on the wall as if to say good-bye to the family birth-place.

Then they flew off to another life and another stormy night.

Rebirth – Cote d'Azur
(Forest fire in the south of France)

When pine trees burn
they can't return
to clothe the slopes in verdant green.
But maquis grows with sweet rock rose,
with rosemary and fragrant myrrh
and scents the breeze with lavender.

By miracle of death and life
new beauty will the hills acquire
above the sparkling emerald sea,
born through the tragedy of fire.

Rosemary Williamson

Diamonds are Forever?
(Cruise Liner Boutique)

She held them high before the light
and viewed the jewels one by one;
the hands were old and wrinkled brown
by years of hot Miami sun.

For riches bring to lonely life
a diamond mask to hide the tears,
a sparkling solace for the soul,
an emerald cloak to shield from fears.

With misty eyes and distant look
she passed her money to the girl –
whose skin was glowing gold with health,
whose lips were rubies, teeth were pearl,
who longed for leisure, ease and wealth

who smiled at her.

Rosemary Williamson

The Inheritance

I had forgotten about this box
and what it contains.
I last saw it thirty years ago
when I was tidying up
and put it away in the roofspace.

When my time has come and then has gone
and my children are filling black bags for the skip
perhaps they will find this and wonder.

A small black and white box and its contents.
Will they shake it and rattle it
and ask what it is?

Perhaps they'll be sorry
when it is opened –
no diamonds, no silver,
not even a watch.

Should I write a short note to put with it?
And say that this ammonite is rare and unique?
That a museum would be proud to display it forever?
And generations would marvel and ponder?

Perhaps I should tell of the strangest events
that led me to find it on the wildest of beaches,
the romance and the mystery that had taken me there.

But I think I'll say nothing at all.
The fossil and its history can die with me
when the box and a binbag unite in a dump.

It is my story, my history, my lodestone or star

Gerry Miller

The Blackbirds of Cinimar Hill
by
Dorothy Pyper

In the midst of farming country Daphne's garden lay like a cake on a cloth of chequered colours. The colour themes of the fields seemed to be represented by each tall tree that grew there. The birds loved it. Every day Daphne began the tending of her garden by feeding the birds. She was very particular about what she gave them in the cold weather, rubbing into the left-over food and breadcrumbs any fat she had saved from cooking. As the weather improved with the year, her enthusiasm waned, but she always nudged it back into performance and served the birds each morning a variety of fruit and suitable kitchen. Some she put on the sky dish outside her window - the rest she spread on the lawn. In return, from February right into the summer the birds sang like divas. Daphne considered it their social contract.

Although the chorus had grown in magnificence each year, one bird stood out from the rest. She heard among the syrupy crooning - a persistent call of a cat and another time a telephone and yet again a horse neighing – until last year, when called phrases seemed to contain her name. Now all the birds had perfected wolf whistles – but she thought her heart would break this year in early May, when suddenly one called her name. She thought her heart had stopped. After that it was easy enough to translate their language with her imagination purring like a Lamborghini. They were in mighty tune.

'Daphne is very nice'. 'I love you da-fi-nee'. She stood up and running to the end of the griselina hedge she looked up and down . No-one was about. A movement at the top of the bird cherry declared a presence. 'Onomatopaeaea' called the maple Crimson King. The eucalyptus gunii responded sharply with a clear wolf whistle. She could hardly believe her ears. Yes, yes she told herself it is real - but even knowing that, she suspected some trickery. She ran to the other end of the garden where the jasmine fronted a wall full of hiding places. Not a soul to be found. She whistled her food whistle in joy. A chorus of birds answered her and before she knew it she had joined in and they were responding every time she made a sound. So she carried another batch of primulas down to the 'podium' and settling her knees on the cushion she renewed her task of planting, whistling every time there was a lull in the chorus.

'Daf-in-ee is pretty'- this guy sounded like Jim out of Eastenders- 'I love you' – the macrocarpa tree replied. 'Onomatopaeoea' called the acer saccharinum –'I love you too' called Daphne.

She had nearly finished planting when her husband appeared. 'Did you hear, did you hear' she called excitedly . He smiled and knelt beside her.

' I was on the phone with Eugene and he asked me if we had a budgie.'

He helped her to the house later, with their forks and buckets of weeds. A kind of absolute peace seemed to accompany their journey. It seemed that their joy grew with the season as May passed into June and John came home early to join the concert.

The good weather persisted and Daphne became involved in family visits. She had no time to garden until one afternoon, she set out with new plants for the long border in her wheelbarrow. She gave out her food whistle - she clicked her tongue. A robin chirped looking for food. But the silence of the blackbirds was stunning. She tried again and again using different sounds. She thought she saw them - flashes of black among the trees, but there was no sound. Somewhere along the way, the blackbirds had stopped singing. She felt very depressed until by the end of the week she couldn't bring herself to go outdoors. Without the birds the garden had become a foolish retreat. A dread of birds had come upon her place and there was no health in her.

It was the second week in June when she noticed that the blue tits and chaffinches lingered in the bushes, no longer confident in their actions. She realised that a lot more food than they could eat was disappearing. Perhaps the blackbirds had returned. Excitedly, she began a watch. A clattering, a presence and soon she knew the truth. A huge black crow fed and flew off to where she could see another waited. Yelling, she ran out, banging her stick against the door.

John and Daphne kept up their assault for a week, until they awoke to a commotion above. Crows cawed and clucked and something rolled down the tiles. She ran into the garden and saw a huge bird emerging upwards from a disused chimney pipe high on their roof. It expanded in the air to become the biggest crow she'd ever seen. Further along the roof, a grey-headed chick sat in the gutter, it's gleaming blue black feathers glinting in the sun. Slowly it turned its head and looked at her. That night she hardly slept thinking of it yards away in the chimney-pipe.

Next day she rang the local hardware store and she enquired about bird scarers. The girl who answered the call, appeared to have no idea of what she was talking about, but got someone who might know what she meant. Daphne listened and took note of his country knowledge. Bird scarers were no longer in use but she now had several names of firms who might stock them. For two hours she spoke to men who were puzzled by her enquiries. Eventually some bird lover in some store said – 'for crows you need pest control –' get yellow pages'. So she rang the first firm dealing with pests. They took her name and postcode. Their man would call. All that day she suffered the crow noises and tried to forget them by gardening at the long bed. Now the silence was replaced by a cacophany of sounds from the air above and from each tall tree. 'Kaw' called the macrocarpa, 'Keaw-Keaw' answered the acer Crimson King, 'keaw-keaw gobble kluck'came from the acer sacarrhinum , where the wood-pigeon roosted. Daphne shuddered. 'Gyaaa, gyaaah' she screamed worse than any crow. The crows ignored her, flying sedately and strongly in their family groups above their chosen roosts. They had ringed her in. A bloodline of crows had come to the birth of a new chick. Craftily, they went to sleep in her garden, making no noise at all. Only the chimney-pipe clucked.

Next morning she poured out her heart to the pest control man who rang about eight a.m. 'I can no longer live here' she finished.

'It's not a rook' he said of her description of the adult bird 'it's a carrion crow'. She felt herself grow human and womanly again.

'Are those not English?' He assured her that N.I. had carrion crow too and went on to describe a deviation with a streak of white.

'Sounds like a certain post modernist Ulsterman'.
He laughed 'What did the chick look like?' When she'd finished the description, he said 'That's a jackdaw', and went on to assure her of their pestilent ways. He said there was nothing she could do, under a new law all the crow family were protected. Bird scarers needed permission since effective ones scared all the birds.   'It's funny you should be talking of this. Today I awakened to the most wonderful birdsong... I never heard the like of it before –and it all came from one bird'. He told her where he lived. Her heart lifted – he'd found a new chick to love.

'That's my musical director' she cried, 'you're only one hill away. That's not far for a bird.' Daphne felt joy rising like fizzy lemonade.

''I'll give you a wave sometime' the man said.

For several days, John and Daphne noticed an absence of crows. They saw an occasional bird flying to the roof, either to feed or to check on the weakly clucking chimney-pipe. It seemed that all the crows in the district were following Wilmer Bryce's thresher. Then - amazingly - Daphne saw a new chick at the bottom of her lawn, and was shocked to realise that she felt relief that it had not died in the pipe. It was joined by a second . Briefly they referred to each other, then as if dancing a gavotte, they began to walk towards the house. Each step they took registered pleasure and newness as if they were celebrating life.

'Like clerical gentlemen with gout' said John. When the third chick joined the dance, Daphne pulled the curtains over the window - she realised that they could no longer have the garden of their dreams, with impresario blackbirds as friends. They had to admit all the other birds. If the jackdaws left then the carrion crows might return – their kin selection meant that they created the street community, not the garden owners. She handed John a holiday brochure.

'Let's pack' she said 'before they all start breeding again.'

Footnote. Daphne and John returned to their home two weeks later. Within days the garden was filled with blackbirds of different ages and sizes scooting around the ground at feeding time acting like soldiers under fire. Miraculously, the crows had gone – all but one, which made a solo visit to walk the length of the lawn, to look at Daphne and to fly away never to be seen again. (Next time he'd come by a different route.)

Old World War I Soldier 'Hard Times'

When young I remember old men (some without limbs) begging in the streets of Belfast. One sat, his one leg outstretched, crutch parallel to that leg, his cap in front hoping to receive a few coppers. It was well known he was a first war veteran. I, like the rest, usually rushed past him. Welfare in those days was not as charitable. With hindsight I wish that I and others had given more consideration to his plight.

He sits alone, does anyone care?
With his haggard look, life has been unfair.
On the cold pavement, his one leg outstretched.
The other one gone, to him this is no sketch.

He never speaks, just staring ahead.
With a vacant look that leaves so much unsaid.
What memories disturb him, no one can tell.
He came back, while many others fell.

His crutch beside him, greasy cap out in front.
He does not ask, people give what they want.
It is never much, a few pence at a time.
But it helps to sustain, in his life of grime.

Most people rush by and don't see him there.
But a faithful few always seem to care.
The ones who rush, if only they'd pause,
They would see a person, not a lost cause.

The debt that is owed, no one can tell.
To men like him, that came through hell.
They deserved better, than sitting to beg,
Alone in their memories, with only one leg.

Tom Jamison

Not Just For Christmas
by
Yvonne Young

Suddenly, it's dark – a silence falls across the room. Is it possible? Just a few short moments ago there was excitement and bustle in the room. "Set this here!" "No, that goes there!" "That's better!" a hushed voice exclaimed. Another voice asked, "Is that it all? Are we finished?" There was such an air of, of, of what? Expectation? Yes! Expectation! Gradually, I peeped open my eyes, it was really dark, so dark I couldn't see my hand before my face. "Oh wait, that's better," I thought. There was a warm glow coming from the embers in the fireplace, a very soft, dim glow. Relief flooded over me, and I looked around. "Oh, how wonderful." Everywhere I looked there were toys. "Where am I?" I thought. "Am I in a toyshop?" I asked aloud. "Toyshop? Toyshop?" a deep voice asked. "What do you mean, a Toyshop?" "Don't you know what night this is?" asked the voice. "Nnn…no sir, I am sorry sir!" I answered, looking round to see who had spoken. There was a funny shuffling noise and I looked over to where the sound was coming from. In the dim glow I could see the shiny buttons on the coat of a soldier. I gazed at him. "Well, my dear," said the voice, much softer than before, "Let me tell you, it is Christmas Eve." "Ohhh!" I gasped, "Christmas Eve!" I had heard of such a wonderful, magical night before. "When was that?" I was so excited. "Christmas Eve!" I gasped again. "Yippee!" I shouted, as I jumped down off my chair. "Shhhhhhhhh!" chorused an array of voices, "You'll wake the children!" they exclaimed. "Children?" I asked. "Yes, children," again the voices chorused the words. "What children?" I asked. "Ahem," cleared the first voice, "You don't know much!" he added, a little more gently. "There are lots of children in this family, six girls and three boys. Each of us toys has been allocated to one of the children." "Yes," added the other toys, "isn't it exciting?" "Yes," I answered, " but how do we know who belongs to who?"

Giggles echoed around the room. I couldn't see very well, "Who all is here?" I asked   Somewhere, over in the centre of the room there was a sort of noise that I didn't recognise, a sort of whirring, fizzling noise. There was a loud "click" and the room was a blaze of multi-coloured lights. "Ohhh!" I gasped in wonder. "What was this beautiful display in front of me?" It looked like a, a, a tree, but it had all sorts of baubles and beads and even little lanterns and silvery ribbons on it. The soldier smiled as he came towards me. "That, my dear, is a Christmas Tree. Every year the parents in this home decorate a tree for the children. It is all part of the Christmas Celebrations." "Ohhh!" I wondered, "It is sooo beautiful." I gazed at the tree, it was just magical!

"Allow me to introduce myself," said the soldier, "I am Sergeant Sedgewood and I belong to Jonathan. "But," I interrupted, "I'm sorry, I don't understand how you know who you belong to."

Again there were giggles and whispers. Then a beautiful lady danced and twirled into the centre of the floor. "Sedgie really! You are so stuffy. It is really simple, my dear. In this home on Christmas Eve the children hang up their stockings for Father Christmas coming. Each child "claims" a special place for their presents, and that is where Father Christmas and his helpers leave the gifts." "Oh, so that is why I heard voices saying where to put the toys!" "Yes, dear," said the lady dancer," my name is Lady Davinia but my friends call me Dave. I belong to Jane, she is the eldest. This guy here is Sedgie to all of us, and don't be put off by his stuffiness." With that she gave a twirl and playfully bumped Sgt. Sedgewood to the side. "Grmp!" he said, as he straightened his uniform jacket, "That's enough of that." One by one the toys came before me to introduce themselves. There was Daredevil Bill, a motorcyclist who performed "wheelies" on his motorbike. He belonged to Robert, who was second eldest. "Acrobat Ann" tumbled over from her circus tent, while "Walkies Wilma" walked her little brown dog towards me. "Yap! Yap!" he barked, and promptly sat down. "Come on," coaxed Wilma tugging on his lead, "At this rate this'll take all night!" "Acrobat Ann belongs to Elizabeth, while I belong to Alexandra," said Wilma, " We are very pleased to meet you."
"We're over here," whispered some voices. I gazed in their direction. Oh how beautiful! There with her head held high, was a magnificent swan, her wings were up and there appeared to be a seat in her back. She was rocking gently to and fro. Wrapped in a soft pink blanket, nestling between her wings, was a baby doll. She looked so peaceful. "Hello, I am Sasha Swan and my precious cargo is Baby Bonnie. We belong to the twins, Corine and Carol, Baby Bonnie was so tired, I have rocked her to sleep." " You are so beautiful," I breathed, "Isn't this exciting?" "Don't forget about me!" squealed an excited little voice; "I'm sit ' n' ride Jack. I'm a train. Choo! Choo!" "Sshh, Jack!" everyone chorused, "the children!" "Sorreee," moaned Jack, "but just because I'm for baby Richard doesn't mean I should always be last!" "No, Jack, you are right, we're sorry," soothed Lady Davinia, "but this time you are not last, what about Margaret Rose?"
"That's me!" I answered, "I am Margaret Rose and I belong to, to, to…..!" I could feel the tears welling up in my eyes. "I don't know who I belong to." Suddenly an overwhelming sense of loss washed over me. "Don't worry," whispered Lady Davinia, "We know who you are and you are really very special. You belong to Sarah!" "Sarah?" I asked, "who is Sarah, and why am I so special?" "Well, my dear," said Lady Davinia, as the other toys gathered round. "Sarah has been very sad. She is the third eldest and a few years ago Father Christmas brought her a baby doll She called her Susan." There was a sound of sniffs from some of the other toys. "Anyway," went on Lady Davinia, "Sarah really loved Susan. She used to play with her, feed and bath her, she even took her out for walks in her pram, while her mother took the younger children out in their pram. Last year Susan went to visit Father Christmas. When she came back on

Christmas Eve she had a new pram, as well as some new clothes. When Sarah saw her sitting up in her pram on Christmas morning she was delighted. Susan was wearing a lovely new blue coat and the prettiest of dresses. It was yellow, Sarah's favourite colour, with little pink rosebuds on it. Susan went everywhere with Sarah. Sarah even dreamed about her. One day she shared a dream she had had with her mother. Sarah had dreamed that Susan had climbed out of the pram while they were out for a walk, smiled up at Sarah, took her hand and walked along beside her. She just loved that dream and often talked about it. "Oh," I gasped; I just felt there was a but coming, yet I wasn't prepared for what I heard next. "One day Sarah put Susan outside in the garden in her pram. She said it was time for Susan's nap, just like her twin sisters had a nap time." It was a beautiful day, Sarah was inside for quite a long time. She was helping her mother, brothers and sisters with some chores. There was a rap at the door. It was a street seller, she was selling some clothes pegs and little "rose basket" shaped paper packets with sewing needles inside. Sarah's mum bought some sewing needles and the street seller went away. Later on, when they had finished their chores, Sarah went out into the garden to bring Susan indoors. She couldn't believe her eyes, Susan was gone, and the doll pram was empty. Oh, dear, dear, it was so sad." Lady Davinia stopped talking for a few minutes; she blew her nose, and wiped her eyes. I had such a lump in my throat, too. I swallowed hard. "So, am I here to replace Susan?" I asked. "Oh no, my dear," Lady Davinia gulped, " No dear, no-one could ever replace Susan. You are here to help Sarah to love again. It is a challenge, but you must be yourself, we believe you were hand picked just for Sarah, and she will grow to love you too. Isn't that right everyone?" Everyone nodded in agreement," Yes," they whispered, "Sarah needs you!"

Well, I thought, so that was why I hadn't known before I arrived who I belonged to. So many thoughts were racing through my head, questions, lots of questions. My heart was pounding in my chest. Would Sarah be disappointed in me? Would she want me? Would I be stolen, too? Suddenly, my thoughts are back to today, I am about to celebrate another Christmas. This one, however, will be very different. I am fifty years old now, my curls are a little bit less bouncy than they used to be, and my eyelashes have become quite thin. I sit in a pretty new dress, this time made by Sarah. An air of excitement rules this home. What is it? Well, Sarah's little grandson is coming to visit, what a bundle of energy and fun he is! It doesn't matter that I am a girl's toy, he is fascinated by me and loves to play with me. I am as excited as Sarah is at his impending visit. So here I sit, reminiscing over my life, not just with Sarah, but also with her daughter, now all grown up, too, but that is another story.

Superstition
(I looked up)

O why did I look up
to see that slender silver sliver of a moon
through glass?

The February air was sharp,
the evening sky of gently lightning hue
as winter afternoon extends its light
hinting of spring and life and all things new.

It brings bad luck, they say,
to see a new born moon
this way,
but then I think – no longer sad -,
thank God that I have had
another precious day of life.

It can't be true.

Rosemary Williamson

The Thing I Hate
(an obsession)

We approach like boxers to a fight
within the ring of glowing screen.
My hackles rise, like scorpion's tail,
Striking with fingers on qwerty keys
I write, make commands with mouse.
But, perverse thing, you frustrate my intent.
I rage, you glow, consuming words.
I shall have my way, with skill
Defeat your wiles and impose my will,
For you have cost me much, so persevere I must
And though it chokes me to say 'compromise'.
This must I do to achieve my aim.
To create prose and poetic verse
And send them to the internet.

Ray Heath

Felicity's New Clothes
by
Eirene Armstrong

The sexton's family lived in the little cottage adjoining the graveyard. There were eight children in all, making it a hard job for their father to provide for them. His wife, Mrs Fielding, was as diligent as himself in striving to keep the old church cleaned, polished and sufficiently warmed for the comfort of the congregation.

It was back-breaking work but the sexton meekly accepted all the additions to his grave-digging and bell-ringing, such as concerts and committee meetings, often late into the night. In those far-off days of the nineteen twenties jobs were hard to find and wages were poor. The dread of each hard pressed family was unemployment because there was little or no help from the state. The main source of assistance for the Fieldings was the kindly old rector with his gifts of cast-off clothing and assistance from church funds. Thanks to his attentiveness the Fieldings managed to be adequately fed and clothed and even to have extra food for celebrations at Christmas, Easter and suchlike.

Entertainment for families then was supplied by the local people in the way of concerts and plays, and often by performances by the pupils in the little nearby church school. Props for such things were borrowed from the rectory, and it was on the morning after a concert that the sexton and his wife were clearing up and cleaning out the school. Mrs Fielding placed several borrowed items in a wheelbarrow and instructed her ten-year-old daughter Felicity to return them to the rectory.

Felicity, delighted at this more pleasant task than the usual ones assigned to her, hastened away with the wheelbarrow. She knew that there would be a mug of milk and a slice of cake dispensed in the rectory kitchen. Consigning Felicity to the care of the maid, the rector's wife instructed her to wait in the kitchen until she returned. This Felicity was only too pleased to do.

Warmed by the fire she munched her cake, drank her milk, and wondered at the abundance of food around her. Hams hung from the ceiling with bunches of herbs and onions. Jars of bottled fruit, honey and jam winked at her from the dresser. The well-fed cat and dog snoozed contentedly on a rug before the range and Felicity felt a pang of envy for their easeful lives. Her short life had been dominated by school and the endless tasks assisting her parents in their demanding work.

All too soon the rector's wife returned and explained that there were some things in the wheelbarrow to take home with her. Felicity's eyes gleamed as she grasped the handles and glimpsed the clothing within. She was far too wise to go straight home with it for she knew her greedy siblings would pounce and fight over the contents.

Alongside the rectory garden was a leafy lane overhung with trailers of honeysuckle and wild roses, excellent for concealment. Birds fluttered around but Felicity scarcely noticed the variety of song that accompanied her efforts to examine and sort the clothing. She enjoyed handling the beautiful silks and soft cottons as she tried the dresses on, one by one, though they swamped her small frame. There she pirouetted and preened among the honeysuckle and wild roses. She knew that she must lay claim to the prettiest garment on the grounds that she had been the one to carry out the errand. After a struggle she fixed on a pretty silk dress in a cream colour patterned in blue and yellow roses. Stuffing this under her cardigan she proceeded home with the barrow. There the little Fieldings fell upon the clothes as well as the substantial cake and pot of honey that were also supplied.

But the clothes had to be cut down and remade to fit the children.

All night long Mrs Fielding plied her needle and scissors so that by the morning each little Fielding had a new garment in which to attend school. The pupils were less attentive than usual. Covetous and knowing little faces surveyed the Fieldings. It was not until lunchtime when the pupils were released to the playground and out of reach of the cane that they were able to give full vent to their feelings.

Surrounding the Fielding children they taunted, "Yiz are poor. Yiz are poor. Yiz have to wear the rectory clothes.'

But Felicity, resplendent in her flower-bedecked cream silk, rose above the taunts, and, confident in glorious superiority over all, perched on the school wall and looked disdainfully down.

Be Nice to your Home-help
by
Jean Hinds

Your home-help is a humble person, not above getting her hands dirty.

When she rings the bell greet her with a smile, making her feel that you are glad to see her.

Offer her a cup of tea and have a chat, catching up on any news or gossip.

Leave her alone to get on with the chores.

Make sure she gets a break and make a friend of her.

When she finishes don't check the time.

Remember to pay her.

Show her to the door and tell her you are looking forward to seeing her again.

Real Life Stories
by
Jean Galway

Have I been born 70 years too early? I ask myself.

The answer is "No." I have enjoyed what most modern people would call austere years. Rural life is fascinating now, and even more then. Monday was always wash day for the main wash and lasted all morning. There was usually a snack lunch made up from the leftovers of Sunday's dinner. If there was a baby his or her clothes were washed each day. It was a great pride for the mother to have a line of snow white terry towelling nappies blowing in the breeze. "What were they like?" I hear my grand-daughter say. She just goes to the store and buys a big bulky parcel of disposable ones, which have to be got rid of after use.

This brings me back to our wee farm, where most of the animals were pets. I'm not sure if this was a good thing. There were more tears shed over a lamb going to market, than would have been shed over a neighbour's demise. I remember a neighbour had a sheep which lost her lamb at birth. My Dad had an extra lamb so my brother and sister set off with the little orphan lamb to the neighbours. The farmer's wife was delighted rewarding them with apples and biscuits, but the parting was to come. Tears and sobs started, so the lady being kind hearted could not accept so great a sacrifice and the lamb was sent back with them. Dad wasn't best pleased, as pet lambs are hard to rear, but the lamb grew into a healthy sheep, which was consolation.

Then the day the pigs had to be killed was a dreaded day for us. The minute the pig killer arrived we were off like scalded cats to a distant field. We did not intend to starve and took lunch in our pockets. When we thought everything would be over, we came home to find the pig sty quiet and empty and a row of dead carcases awaiting the van to take them to the bacon factory. Farming was hard work and we were almost self sufficient, growing our own grain, potatoes, and having cows, sheep, hens and the above mentioned pigs. One day my husband heard a lady talking to a farmer who said, "You farmers are all the same, always girning about something." "I don't know what you would do without farmers," he replied "Where would you get your vegetables and potatoes?" "Easy ," she said. "Out of the shop." I wonder where she thought the shop got them in the first place.

I can't remember ever being bored. We made our own playthings. I wonder does anyone remember making stilts, with two empty syrup tins threaded with strong cord, home made carts from apple boxes and old pram wheels, kites from strong brown paper, which we printed bright colours? We played all kind of ball games and skipping ropes were in great demand. There were very few obese children then.

My fondest memory was of the sweet shop near our school, run by a lady who must have had the patience of Job. She stocked a wide variety of sweets. Barley sugar sticks, liquorice sticks in bags of sherbet, acid drops, pear drops and multi coloured gobstoppers to name some favourites. She would stand patiently waiting till our mind was made up and our half penny or penny changed hands. Very often the gobstoppers won. They started off deep purple fading to mauve, pink and white as one sucked. Part of the pleasure was bringing the sweet in and out of our mouths to check its progress, not very hygienic, but great fun, with no dire results. All this about sweets has made me feel quite nostalgic. Oh dear, I do hope there is a toffee left in the tin!

Reality Living

We all have seen the glossy ads
that take us on the no-frill flights
to cities of our choice.

Many would agree a long weekend with sangria, sun and sea
is better than the same expense for clotted cream and scones and tea
and rain and wind and fish and chips and sand with everything.

You can sample Barcelona with its cocktail bars and beaches
or Paris with the Eiffel Tower and Moulin Rouge and peaches
or Prague with all its history and its special classic features.

The Szechenyi spa in Budapest is amazing to behold.
Where locals play chess in water to their necks from dawn to dusk
while minerals cure their aches and pains and give them skins of hide.

One of the pools has jets of water to massage the body
and a whirlpool to sweep the swimmers round and round in a vortex
that defies their best endeavours to escape and everyone shrieks.

I used to love the power of that current and tried with the best of them
to swim against the force that does not last too long
and so you know that every thing will turn out to be well.

I do not like it now at all
with its harnessed power
of potential tsunami swell.

Gerry Miller

Out-takes
by
Eddie Whiteside

I know a man who owns a cinema. Now, I'm not talking about your giant
multi-screens, or cineplexes, capable of holding a thousand people. Oh no.
I'm talking about a sixty seater barn conversion in the back garden, a
veritable labour of love conversion, a lifetime's passion conversion, a
dream come true conversion.

There was a time when public cinemas seemed in terminal decline, and
seats, projectors, screens and other paraphernalia were going for a song.
This was Noel's opportunity. He snapped up bargain after bargain to
create what I could only describe as a Victorian time capsule at the back of
his house in Comber.

I've been in it a few times, and every time I enter I feel I've returned to my
cosy childhood, when my parents took me to the pictures. Wolfman,
Dracula, Creatures from Outer Space, and the Thing from the Black
Lagoon glower down threateningly at you from old black and white
posters. Newsreels are from fifty years ago, introduced by a cockerel
crowing, and the ceiling is embellished with ornate carvings. There is even
a toilet off the main viewing auditorium. However, should you wish to
view a modern film you have only to ask the friendly proprietor.

A short time ago, my wife and I were invited, as wedding guests, to go
there one evening to watch the film 'The Father of the Bride.' This was
quite a novel idea and we thought it an excellent alternative to the usual
evening activity at weddings nowadays, of noisy discos where you can
hardly hear yourself think.

The lights were already dimmed when we went in, and after stumbling
down a narrow row of seats, standing on feet other than our own, shoving
our backsides into the faces of seated guests and apologising profusely all
the while, we eventually found our allocated places near the back. They
were not good seats.

Directly in front of me was a huge, balding man with big ears, who
constantly rolled his large head, making it difficult for me to even see the
screen. He seemed to be having breathing problems as well, wheezing and
panting and snorting a lot.

As my eyes gradually accustomed to the dark, he slowly metamorphosed
into a massive Pyrenean Mountain dog. I let out a gasp, which produced
an elbow in the ribs from my neighbour, who whispered that it was the
bride's dog, that she had no-one to look after it, that I was not to worry as
it was a clever dog and very well behaved.

Well, I ask you. Have you ever had to look over the top of a big dog's head
and try to concentrate on a film? I was more worried about it wanting a
pee, and I was pretty sure that, no matter how clever he said it was, it
couldn't read the TOILET sign glowing in green letters at the side. For
some reason I never did learn, it was carried out after about ten minutes,

much to my relief and perhaps to its, for it didn't seem to be enjoying the film much, anyhow.

It was then that the crying started. The bride, still wearing her wedding dress, who had with great difficulty squeezed into the seat in front of my wife, suddenly burst out into tears. She was from eastern Europe and her parents had been unable to attend the wedding, so maybe the choice of film had not been such a good idea after all. Anyway, she was carried out behind the dog.

We had a great view of the film after that.

The Ironing Board
by
Jean Hinds

Molly was married in the seventies and among the many presents they received was an ironing board. She ironed everything – as you do when you are first married.

At first there were only the two of them. After a couple of years there were three and then four in the family.

Baby clothes, school clothes and work clothes all kept the iron and the ironing board very busy.

Then the children left home and once again there were just the two of them.

Thirty-four years after the wedding the marriage fell apart and on the day she left the marital home the ironing board fell apart as well.

Molly stood in her new flat and cried, the ironing board in pieces in her hands.

It had been a very emotional day for her and she wondered whether, like herself, the ironing board had just collapsed from exhaustion after all the years of hard work.

Then, drying her eyes, she thought – stop feeling sorry for yourself. You have a son and a daughter and two lovely grandchildren.

Molly has bought herself a new ironing board and does ironing (which she loves) for a young family.

She knows that half her life is over but the rest is still to come – and she is going to enjoy it.

Sea and Tide

Its greatest fascination are its moods. Always respect it.

I am the master of all shores.
Loved by some, feared by others.
At times looked upon in awe.
By the wise, always respected.

My mood swings are beyond my control.
They are decided over a wide spectrum.
From a signal in the heavens:- 'The Moon'.
To 'El Nino' generated off the Latin American coast.

These factors along with the wind and atmosphere,
Decide how I shall behave on the day.
I am indifferent whether I be wild or serene,
I react as destiny dictates I must.

Since time immemorial mankind has been drawn to me.
Some in great ships, others in small boats.
Each has their reason for being with me.
Hoping if necessary to live with my wrath.

Many unfortunates have been lost to my vile moods,
While others bask in my calmness and light winds.
This shall always be the pattern of sea and tide.
I shall always be here, mankind will always challenge me.

Tom Jamison

The Right Place at the Right Time
by
Jean Hinds

The twenty-seventh of December in the year 2000 saw the first snow of the winter. It was soft and deep but Jane decided to brave the weather and take her two dogs for their daily walk.

It was lovely crunching down the thick snow as they walked in the middle of the road with no cars, lorries, buses or bicycles – just their own foot marks. There was something special about walking on the newly fallen snow, a bit like being the first man on the moon.

Their first stop was at the vet's to buy some worming tablets, then home through Tullycarnet Park.

It was simply beautiful and so peaceful, with no-one about and the dogs enjoying their romp in the snow.

As Jane walked along the hidden path she noticed some movement in a little pocket in the snow and the dogs came bounding over to see what she had found.

Jane picked it up and it was barely alive. Its webbed feet told her that it was a tiny duck. Quickly she put it in the pocket of her coat to keep it warm and headed back to the vet's where she handed it over to the assistant. If she had the car with her she would have taken it to Castle Espie where her husband worked. However as she walked home she felt very proud that she had done her good deed for the day.

When hubby came home that evening she started to tell him her story. "Yes, the bird was handed to me to look after", he said. "They said that a woman found it in Gilnahirk but I didn't know it was you".

Jane went every day to see the little duck which was kept in a warm glass case until it was fully recovered and then it was released into the wild.

Jane felt quite smug for a long time after that, each time she was cooking chicken (not duck) for dinner.

Writing leads

At various workshops members were given the opening lines of a story and invited to write the next section.   The idea was to illustrate how our minds react differently to the same stimuli.
A number of the pieces appear below for you to read and think about. How would you have continued the stories?

Life
Tears welled up in her eyes as she saw the baby for the first time.   So this is my beautiful great-grandson, she thought.   What will life hold in store for him? If I am spared long enough to tell him some of the stories from my youth when he is old enough to understand, what will he make of it all?   Where should I start?
Perhaps I will tell him about…

1

…. my early schooldays – his will be so different from mine.   I will be sure to mention that I didn't start school until I was six years old and I had to walk about a mile to get there. I feel that he will be a little envious when he hears of all the fun that I had on the way there and on the way home in the afternoon.   On wet days I was soaked, which wasn't so nice, but the teacher draped our coats over the fireguard and that both blocked out the heat from the stove and filled the room with the horrible smell of steam from wet clothes.

The winters were colder then, with heavier frost and more snow. Our parents sent money to buy coals to keep the two stoves burning and that was the only source of heat.

I will remember to tell him of the pond beside the school which used to freeze over.   At dinner time some of us decided that it would make a good skating rink. We were having a great time when I – not being very adventurous and standing only a couple of feet from the edge of the pond – heard the ominous cracking of the ice. I leapt to firm ground. The other half dozen pupils were not so lucky and got knickers, underpants and socks soaked as they slid into the icy water.

We all had to face the teacher, which was frightening mainly because we should not have left the playground.

The fireguard was well draped with dripping clothes that day, but thankfully none of them were mine.

Jean Galway

2

.... the first time I held his grandfather in my arms – my beautiful brown-eyed son. The 'bubble of joy' that started somewhere beneath my breasts and swelled within me until it burst through my being, causing hot tears accompanied by strong laughter to escape from me.

I could feel the tears rolling down my cheeks, bringing me back to the here and the now. Hastily I looked around the room which was filled with happiness and laughter.

'Thank goodness no-one has noticed,' I thought, 'the musings of a soft-hearted old woman. 'Mind you, dearest child, I wasn't always the shaky old woman in front of you now. What can you see, little one? Can you see behind these fading brown eyes? Can you see the young girl playing with her friends, splashing in the sea, squealing with joy as the waves break against her legs? Can you see the blushing young girl who looks upon the young man whom she hopes will become her husband?'

Suddenly the baby in my arms starts to cry – a fretful, anguished cry. The room falls silent and my grandson moves swiftly to my side.

'Hush, hush, you are alright'....

Yvonne Young

3

.... the time when a terrible war raged. How as a small child I cowered beneath the staircase listening to the awful uproar of bombs falling and guns blasting. Then the time of great happiness when I went with my mother and sister to stay with elderly relatives in the country. Peace and tranquillity reigned there and I forgot about war. I loved the farm animals, the wild flowers and all the wonders of the countryside.

Even the little overcrowded school at Ballydorn was fascinating. I was used to a huge impersonal Belfast school where the cane was wielded – but there was no cane in this little country school. The two ladies in charge were friendly and sympathetic to the Belfast children and I remember it as a time of great happiness.

I loved to wander through fields with great carpets of poppies, cornflowers, ox-eye daisies, corn marigolds.

Now the fields are all uniformly gold. Even when the corn was reduced to stubble, scarlet pimpernels, heartsease and other such tiny flowers flourished. I learnt their names together with those of the birds and the butterflies.

On wet days there was the swing in the barn and a slide on the rick-shifter.

Every evening about six o'clock the two plough horses returned from their day's toil. James came quietly with the farmer but Charles always insisted on remaining at the top of the hill. When he saw everyone ready and waiting he came racing down the hill and thundering into the yard.

Eirene Armstrong

Changes
He could not believe the change which confronted him. He had to look
closely a second time to make sure that this was the same person. Gone
were the old features which had made his life-long friend instantly
recognisable. A whole new personality surrounded the individual whom
he thought he could have described down to the last detail.

1

Guilt flooded over him like a tide as he walked out to meet his old friend.
His mind travelled back to the day they had parted company and the
dreams they had shared before that fateful day. They had planned to join
the army together but when it came to the final push he simply could not
do it. He would never forget the look on his friend's face when he told
him that he was not going.
Then he heard about the landmine, but nobody could tell him how serious
the injuries were. Now the evidence was in front of him. The injuries
were horrific.
To meet him again was like a dark cloud melting away. He would do
what he could to help. As company director he had the financial clout to
ease the suffering.

Tom Jamison

2

The hair colour was the first thing that made an overwhelming
impression. Gone the sensible and shining locks – a dark bob – and in
their place a bangle of golden curls.
Gone also were the dark-rimmed spectacles which formerly had enhanced
the intellectual and studious appearance. Presumably contact lenses had
been acquired during his six-month absence on a fellowship to China.
Some really concentrated dieting and exercise must have been employed
as the stodgy figure had been superseded by one of svelte and slim
outline. Makeup previously not employed had been applied skilfully to
cheeks, lips and eyes. And as for the style – a clingy red gown and high
stilettos ….
'Hello', she said. 'I've just called to say that I don't feel that I am cut out to
be in charge of this parish…'

Rosemary Williamson

3

Instead of a fierce and rather frightening grimace there was a calm serenity
which had not been there before. The wild and unkempt hair was now
neatly trimmed and carefully combed. A twinkle in the eyes replaced the
earlier intense and penetrating stare. The angular cheekbones were quite
concealed by a healthy covering of flesh.
'I am so glad you have come', he said and smiled at me.
The change had quite unnerved me. What on earth had happened?

Gerry Miller

4

His friend of many years, Henry Harkness, had just returned from a
holiday in India. It was the summer of 2001 and the heat in the sub-
continent had been stifling. Everyone, even the natives, complained and
tried every way to combat the high temperatures.

Henry Harkness was tall, dark and handsome and very mature, the kind
of man any woman would take a second look at and some would surely
swoon over. He was good-looking, fresh and lively, and his smile was
engaging and warm.

He had left Henry at the airport on his departure and was there to meet
him on his return two months later.

How his appearance had changed. One side of his face had dropped.
Now he had two faces. The left side of his face had collapsed, the muscles
had flopped and were dead without expression. The other side was the
normal Henry he knew. There was a disfigured Henry on one side and the
Henry he knew on the other.

On a journey by train across the vast plains of India, unwittingly Henry
had sat by the open window and fallen asleep. The draft of air which had
eased the unbearable heat had also killed the nerve on that side of his face.
Henry had Bell's Palsy.

Billy Fitzell

5

He was no longer the man who had been the professor of literature at the
university – the gentle, vague professor. Now he saw before him a hard-
featured and determined man with ruthless cold blue eyes, a man with the
ability to make terrible decisions of life and death.

He sighed as he looked at the image of himself in the mirror. Perhaps
after the war he would go back to the university and become once more
that rather vague and preoccupied professor of literature. That young
idealist.

No, never, he thought.

That man had died somewhere along the long hard road that he had
travelled. At Krakow or Kotoursky… or one of those places. He couldn't
remember the precise place but he could remember the exact occasion. It
was when he had lost Orina?… it was then.

He had betrayed her and abandoned her. Of course, he had to. The
whole organisation was in danger at the time. He had responsibilities to
the resistance movement. One has to sacrifice a soldier in a war – every
commander knows that. But she had been someone special.

His face hardened. She had been just a soldier sacrificed in the war.

As he looked in the mirror he knew that he could never return to what he
had been.

Ray Heath

6

The 'cold turkey' had been a harrowing experience, far far worse than he had been led to believe. The withdrawal symptoms had left him curled up in the foetal position, yelling and howling like an animal in the corner of his tiny cell, alternately threatening and begging for some relief. He had banged his head on the wall repeatedly, anything to bring a modicum of relief from this living hell.

All semblance of dignity had long passed – bloodied head, dribbling lips, nose a fountain of green slime oozing down his shirt.

And yet, somewhere in the deepest recesses of his mind he fleetingly glimpsed the face of his child, the only person for whom he was prepared to go through this living hell.

Eddie Whiteside

7

I had known John some thirty years ago. Gone was the dapper youth and here was this elderly man. I looked carefully and yes, the brown eyes were the same and I could detect the twinkle and the mischief still lurking in them. But could it be? Was this elderly round-shouldered man with hollow cheeks and gaunt features the same John whom I had known so long ago?

Jean Galway

8

Where there had been an openness and directness in the dark brown eyes Carl now saw a kind of secretiveness, almost a furtive look, which was most uncharacteristic of the Victor he had known since childhood. Allied with this change was an overall shiftiness of manner expressed in involuntary glances behind him, and a hunching of the shoulders that suggested something close to fear.

'Good to see you again, old friend', Carl managed, wanting to prolong this chance meeting but sensing that Victor was uneasy and keen to be on his way. 'Have you time for a chat about old times over a coffee – or perhaps a cognac?'

Noel Spence

9

'We can network the world!'

He had become a word terrorist, wielding his pen to link metaphors and bind us together.

His eyes flashed with inspiration as he said 'Do it! Do it now and I will select!'

Then the old self emerged briefly, his lashes sweeping downwards as doubt momentarily swept over him.

'But only if you want to!'

Dorothy Pyper

Credits and Publications

Jean Galway   2 Collections of published stories and anecdotes
'Snippets of my Yesterdays' and *'The Way Things Were'*
Poems in various anthologies by Anchor Books.

Gerry Miller   *'Awakening'* collection of Poetry (2003) ISBN 0-9548251-0-1
'The World is Getting Smaller' is one of five illustrated poems in Belfast
Metrobus 'Poetry in Motion' series.
'Memories of Bangor 1939-1945' ISBN 1-89898820-X
Poems in various anthologies by Forward Press

Dorothy Pyper   Plays –*'Half-a-Loaf"* (1986), *'A Feast upon You'* (1988)
'Demeter's Granddaughters' (1990), *'Being Culture in the Pig-House'* (2001),
'Upon our Hills' (1998)   Short Stories include *'My Own Place'* in Ards
Writings Publication (1991), *'From the Pig-House'* (1998)
Poetry, monologues and extracts of stories performed with Belfast
(Worker) Writers' Group, Glen Community Association and others

Noel Spence
2 Collections of Short Stories *'Secrets'* and *'Lies and Luck'*
ISBN 0 9548251-1-X
Collection of Poetry 'Bluebells in a Jar (2006) ISBN 0 955548251-2-8

Eddie Whiteside
'Tunnel Vision' was selected for the B.B.C. series 'My Story' and published
in the Belfast Telegraph.
'A Rat's Revenge' was second in an international competition by Bank Street
Writers' Group and published by them.

Rosemary Williamson
2 Collections of Poetry and Reflections *'Butterflies'* and *'More Butterflies'*
Poems and articles have also appeared in the Presbyterian Herald,
Women's Institute Magazine, East Belfast Historical Society Journl, Ulster
Teachers' Union Magazine, 'Poetry Now' Anthology of the W.I., and
British Pastimes Anthology. Rosemary has also given a talk in the B.B.C.
'My Place' series.